PRAISE FOR

DIY **Nut Milks,**
Nut Butters & More

"Melissa King is a healthful treat genius. I stumbled upon her website for a wholesome dessert recipe to make with my son. That first recipe, and every other one I've tried since, have not only been over-the-top delicious, but also nutritious. She does a delightful job of combining the two."
—IVY LARSON, author of *Clean Cuisine* and founder of CleanCuisine.com

"*DIY Nut Milks, Nut Butters & More* is an essential resource for anyone who wants to eat well, go homemade, and make the most of an amazing ingredient. Strawberry Brazil Nut Milk, Cinnamon Pecan Butter, Almond Joy Cookies (!)—I could go on and on. Whether you're just beginning to make more homemade staples or you've been making nut milk for years and want to take it to the next level, Melissa King has you covered."
—ALANA CHERNILA, author of *The Homemade Pantry* and creator of EatingFromTheGroundUp.com

"*My Whole Food Life* is the perfect place to find healthy, easy, and delicious recipes of all kinds—from savory to sweet, and soups to ice cream! Melissa is a magician in the kitchen when it comes to creating wholesome, vibrant, and simple food for everyone to enjoy. If you're interested in exploring the exciting flavors and colors of healthy food then this book is an essential in your home."
—EMILY von EUW, author of *Rawsome Vegan Baking* and creator of ThisRawsomeVeganLife.com

"Like her blog, *My Whole Food Life*, Melissa King's first book is filled with original recipes that are far from intimidating and contain only the purest ingredients. Melissa has taken a familiar ingredient, nuts, and transformed these plants into unique, exciting, flavorful possibilities. These recipes allow home cooks to embrace nutrition *and* create delicious food—it's a win-win! This is more than a cookbook. It is a kitchen manual for anyone who wants to incorporate, and indulge in, plant-based food."
—ASHLEY COX, raw vegan chef and creator of TheNakedFoodLife.com

"When I tested [the Chocolate Almond Banana Cups] in the Bauer house this past weekend everyone FLIPPED OUT! Best part? There's only 5 ingredients and the recipe's super-simple to whip together."
—JOY BAUER, *Today* show host and founder of Joy Bauer Nutrition

THE EXPERIMENT

BECAUSE EVERY BOOK IS A TEST OF NEW IDEAS

D0311473

DIY Nut Milks, Nut Butters & More

FROM ALMONDS TO WALNUTS

MELISSA KING

THE EXPERIMENT

NEW YORK

The Experiment, LLC
220 East 23rd Street, Suite 301
New York, NY 10010-4674
www.theexperimentpublishing.com

This book contains the opinions and ideas of its author. It is intended to provide helpful and informative material on the subjects addressed in the book. It is sold with the understanding that the author and publisher are not engaged in rendering medical, health, or any other kind of personal professional services in the book. The author and publisher specifically disclaim all responsibility for any liability, loss, or risk—personal or otherwise—that is incurred as a consequence, directly or indirectly, of the use and application of any of the contents of this book.

The Experiment's books are available at special discounts when purchased in bulk for premiums and sales promotions as well as for fund-raising or educational use. For details, contact us at info@theexperimentpublishing.com.

Library of Congress Cataloging-in-Publication Data

King, Melissa (Melissa G.)
DIY nut milks, butters & more : from almonds to walnuts / Melissa King.
   pages cm
   ISBN 978-1-61519-230-4 (pbk.) -- ISBN 978-1-61519-231-1 (ebook) 1. Cooking (Nuts) 2. Nut products. I. Title.

TX814.K56 2014
641.6'45--dc23

                                                    2014018590

ISBN 978-1-61519-230-4
Ebook ISBN 978-1-61519-231-1

Cover design by Susi Oberhelman
Cover photographs by Melissa King
Text design by Pauline Neuwirth, Neuwirth & Associates, Inc.

Manufactured in China
Distributed by Workman Publishing Company, Inc.
Distributed simultaneously in Canada by Thomas Allen & Son Ltd.

First printing November 2014
10 9 8 7 6 5 4 3 2

*This book is dedicated to my girls,
Meadow and Olive.*

Contents

Introduction

Welcome to my book! To start things off, I'm going to take you through a brief history of nut milks and nut butters and their respective benefits to your health. I'll also cover the many different types of milks and butters you can make. You're probably already aware of almond milk and peanut butter, but there's so much more to enjoy in these categories—you'll be surprised by the variety.

To help you out in the kitchen, I've included a list of the common ingredients and equipment I use to create my recipes, as well as some valuable tips that will make the process as smooth as, well, butter. I'll then walk you through basic recipes for nut milks and nut butters, along with a few flavor variations that will transport you back to being a kid again. The really fun stuff starts as we delve into some creative, tasty ideas for the milks and

butters we've made—you'll even find recipes that take advantage of any leftover pulp. And, finally, at the end of it all, you can just sit back and enjoy, since the best part of making these recipes is eating the goodies you create.

Why Nut Milks?

Picture a tall, cold glass of milk. Do you simultaneously imagine a cow in a pasture, mooing to her heart's content? Not only is this conjured-up scene from a dairy farm hardly realistic, but it's also difficult to deny the dairy industry's influence on our lives. We pour milk in our coffee and over our cereal. We bake with it. We cook with it. We describe it as *creamy*, *silky*, *velvety*, and *smooth*. Some of us even drink it straight from a carton. From the time we're children, we're told that cow's milk is good for our teeth and bones. Later, we give our own kids milk so that they can grow up to be strong and healthy, never questioning the validity of what the marketers have told us. *I saw it on TV and online, so it must be true!*

I have a question, though: Why do we limit ourselves to dairy? Why *stop* at cow's milk? Almonds, cashews, hazelnuts, pistachios, macadamia nuts, Brazil nuts, and even sunflower seeds can all be made into milks, each with their own qualities of richness, creaminess, silkiness, and nutrition. Moreover, these milks offer us new and exciting alternative flavors to enjoy in our coffee, over cereal, and in our baking. And when you make nut milks at home, you can use the leftover pulp in fun and delicious ways, too—see How to Use Nut Pulp, page 57.

People of Northern European descent have evolved to digest the lactose in cow's milk. It's thought that the practice of consuming nonhuman milk started about 7,500 years ago, with the spread of livestock domestication. In other regions of the world, however, and increasingly in the West, many people are lactose intolerant. Some, like my daughters, are outright allergic to dairy milk (in my daughters' case, this caused severe gastrointestinal issues such as acid reflux). In fact, cow's milk is among the most common allergens in American children. For one reason or another, large numbers of the world's population can't drink dairy milk.

For those who can't consume cow's milk or simply wish to branch out a bit, there are other options, some of which you may have tried already. Soy milk was all the rage for a time, but now people are beginning to shy away from consuming too much of it for a variety of reasons. One factor is the growing concern over genetically modified organisms (GMOs), since more than 90 percent of soy products in the United States are made with GMOs. Some other alternatives, such as rice and oat milks, aren't as versatile as nut milks and lack its desirable creamy quality. In addition, most store-bought milks contain preservatives, thickeners, added sugar, and other natural flavorings to enhance their shelf life, taste, and mouthfeel, not to improve your health.

Nut milks are flavorful and easy to make, rendering them an enjoyable, natural alternative to other milks.

Let's take almond milk, for example. It might seem new to some people, but in medieval times almond milk was a staple in many kitchens, since dairy milk spoiled too quickly. With the advent of refrigeration, though, cow's milk became the go-to ingredient and beverage. In the United States, by the early 2000s, almond milk could be found only in small, niche, health food markets. Recently, however, it has regained popularity as increasingly more people give up dairy and soy. In fact, in 2011 sales of almond milk were up 79 percent from the previous year.

Although we can now go to grocery stores across the country and buy almond milk, hazelnut milk, and the like, most of these commercial variations still contain additives and thickeners to give them a longer shelf life and smoother texture. If you're trying to maintain a clean diet free of preservatives and processed foods, such ingredients will make you want to put these products back on the shelf. I admit, at first I was intimidated by the idea of making nut milk, but I soon had it mastered. With this book, you, too, will grow spoiled by the wide variety of flavors and uses for nuts, and you'll never look at another carton of milk or stick of butter again.

Why Nut Butters?

Here's a classic American scene: a mother making a peanut butter and jelly sandwich as her child looks on fondly, mouth watering, waiting to savor each bite. How did this simple sandwich become such a staple in our culture? The Aztecs were the first people known to grind roasted peanuts into a paste, and by doing so, it seems they created an international sensation that has lasted throughout the ages. Peanut butter gained its fame in the United States during both world wars, when the troops would eat it as an easy-to-carry protein source. In 1928 commercially sold peanut butter made with partially hydrogenated oils—to keep it from separating—hit the market.

Today, peanut butter, along with other forms of nut butter, makes up a nearly $1 billion industry. And while most Americans enjoy this tasty food and clearly spend a lot of money doing so, nut butters are actually quite easy to make at home. If you own a good

blender or food processor and have a few minutes to spare, healty, homemade nut butter can be yours for the taking—and making!

In addition to its incredible flavor, nut butter is good for you: two tablespoons of almost any kind of nut butter contain about 200 calories, a healthy dose of beneficial fats, and anywhere between four and eight grams of protein. Making homemade nut butters also means a food product that's closer to the original source, since you skip the extra processing steps that manufacturers take to keep the butters from separating from the oil and to extend shelf life. You enjoy so many benefits, with the only drawback being having to wash a few dishes.

Types of Nut Milks and Butters

Almost everyone has heard of almond milk and peanut butter, and I've talked about them quite a bit already. These may be, respectively, the best-known variety of nut milk and nut butter, but there are others that are just as appetizing and equally nutritious. In the next few chapters I'll give you some fantastic milk and butter recipes made from a wide range of nuts—macadamias, Brazil nuts, pistachios, hazelnuts, cashews, and, of course, almonds. I've also included recipes using sunflower seeds for those with nut allergies. All of these can also be used to make wonderful desserts and so much more. By the end of this book, you'll be amazed at the many diverse uses of nuts. I hope you enjoy!

Health Benefits of Nut Milks and Butters

Besides tasting oh-so-good, nut milks and nut butters are also chock-full of beneficial nutrients. They're a fine source of omega fatty acids, are high in fiber, are loaded with vitamins and minerals, have no sugar, have zero cholesterol, and, for those who count them, they're low in calories. They seem too good to be true, really. Having all of these virtues means they can help reduce the risk of heart disease, fight cancer, control diabetes, and even aid those with osteoporosis. It's almost silly that nut milks and butters aren't more prevalent. Since I've already mentioned the health benefits of nut butters, let's look at how nut milks stack up against the competition.

CALORIC CONTENT

The caloric content of nut milk is far lower than that of dairy milk. Animal milks are inherently higher in calories, since they are the means of delivering the nutritional needs of growing off-spring. It should go without saying that nut milks need not serve that purpose. So if counting calories matters to you, then nut milks are the way to go. For example, a typical 8-ounce (240 ml) glass of unsweetened almond milk contains only 35 total calories, with 25 of those coming from fat. In contrast, the same amount of organic whole milk contains 150 calories. Even skim milk has about 85 calories. This means that roughly four glasses of nut milk are equal in calories to one glass of whole milk. It also means that all your favorite sweet treats just got that much healthier.

SUGAR- AND CHOLESTEROL-FREE

Did you know that an 8-ounce (240 ml) glass of whole dairy milk can contain up to 35 milligrams of cholesterol? That's a whopping 12 percent of the recommended daily allowance. Skim milk, while lower in fat, still contains cholesterol. Nut milks, on the other hand, are naturally cholesterol-free.

That's great news for people who are genetically prone to high cholesterol, like my husband, who had to give up cow's milk. Nut milks even go a step further, with cholesterol-lowering effects from the vitamin E, magnesium, monounsaturated fats, flavonoids, and omega fatty acids found in them. The flavonoids and omega fatty acids are especially important, because they're known to fight heart disease. The skins, if left on while making nut milk, are full of flavonoids. Plus, homemade nut milk is sugar-free. If you want it sweetened, the amount of sugar that goes into it is up to you. Dairy milk, however, has naturally occurring sugars, and to make skim milk taste better, store-bought brands add sugar to replace the fat that was removed. There's almost no way to avoid sugar in dairy milk.

FIBER-RICH

Fiber aids the digestion process, and, unfortunately, most Americans don't get enough of it in their diet. White flours and many other commercial foods remove fiber during the process-ing procedure, and dairy milk contains no natural fiber. Nut milk, as a plant-based food, contains 1 gram of fiber in an 8-ounce (240 ml) glass. Since most people need between 25 and 38 grams of fiber a day, every little bit helps.

MINERALS AND VITAMINS

Most store-bought milks have been fortified with vitamins and minerals. This is a fancy way of saying that the nutrients were mixed in artificially, because they were either stripped out during processing or were never actually in the food to begin with. It's important to be aware of this. If you think one of the only ways to get the minerals and vitamins you need is to purchase milk from a grocery store, you're wrong. Copper, zinc, iron, magnesium, manganese, calcium, phosphorus, potassium, and selenium can all be found naturally in nuts, which means you can reap the same health benefits by making nut milk at home.

PROTEIN CONTENT

An 8-ounce (240 ml) glass of home-made almond milk contains around 2 grams of protein, which is about four times lower than the equivalent in dairy milk. (The same amount of soy milk normally contains 7 grams of protein.) Although most nut milks have a lower protein content, their other health benefits far outweigh this fact. If you're looking to get more protein through milk, it's easy to add some protein powder to your drink. For those who choose not to consume dairy milk, the protein content of nut milk is higher than that of another common dairy substitute, rice milk. In general, if you're eating a balanced diet, this lower protein content shouldn't be of concern, even if it is worth nothing.

Ingredients

Most of the ingredients used in this book are pretty straightforward, but it's still important to review the following list, since some items might need further explanation. For example, I call for gluten-free oat flour, rolled oats, or steel-cut oats in many of these recipes. If you're sensitive to gluten, you need to make sure that the oats you purchase are certified gluten-free, since oats are often processed in the same factories as wheat. A product should specify whether that's the case, but do check the label to be sure.

You may notice that about 90 percent of these recipes are vegan, with the occasional use of honey. If you're a strict vegan, you can substitute maple syrup for honey in those recipes.

I chose the ingredients that follow because they're either in their natural state, such as the fruits, nuts, seeds, and grains, or they're minimally processed and all-natural, like pure maple syrup and raw honey. You can find many of these ingredients in your local natural foods grocery store or health food market, or you can order them online (see page 187 for a list of Internet retailers for all of the items listed below).

APPLESAUCE

Applesauce can be employed in baking in myriad ways. I often use it as a binder, in place of oil, or to add a natural sweetness to baked goods. I only work with unsweetened applesauce, so I can better control the amount of sugar going into a recipe. Make sure you check label before you buy applesauce, since some brands contain undesirable ingredients.

Applesauce can replace most oils at a 1:1 ratio. However, if you substitute applesauce for all of the oil in a recipe the end product can be slightly gummy.

I like to use at least 1 to 2 tablespoons of oil in my recipes for a better texture. If you're adventurous, you can easily make your own applesauce by grinding up some peeled, sliced apples in a food processor. Try to pick a naturally sweet apple—I like Galas or Honeycrisps.

CACAO POWDER

One great way to add some antioxidants to your nut milks and nut butters is to add a little cacao, which is the raw, unprocessed form of the cocoa bean. Antioxidants, which are abundant in cacao powder, kill free radicals and could help prevent cancer. You can use cacao in powder form or in nibs, which are similar to chocolate chips. Since raw cacao contains no sugar, it's naturally very bitter, so use it sparingly in recipes that are meant to be sweet. If you like dark chocolate, eating cacao won't be a difficult transition.

CHOCOLATE

Some of these recipes call for dark chocolate or chocolate chips. For dark chocolate, I like the 72 percent cacao variety to avoid too much added sugar. Feel free to go with a higher or lower percentage, though—that's just my personal preference. Most of the recipes that include dark chocolate call for 3- or 3.5-ounce (85 or 100 g) bars. You can buy high-quality varieties at many grocery stores these days; I use Endangered Species Chocolate bars in my baking.

For chocolate chips, I'm fond of the brand Enjoy Life, since they're gluten-, dairy-, and nut-free. They do, however, contain a small amount of processed sugar. You can also use carob chips, which are only mildly sweet, although I find they don't work as well as chocolate chips in recipes that require melted chocolate.

If none of these chocolate choices fits in with your lifestyle, you can also make your own. Just mix together ½ cup (120 ml) of coconut oil, ½ cup (60 g) of cocoa or cacao powder, and 2 to 3 tablespoons of pure maple syrup. You can even pour the melted chocolate mixture into molds to make your own chocolate bars!

COCONUT MILK

Coconut milk is often found in vegan ice creams and rich soups. It's thick and velvety, making it the perfect dairy-free alternative to heavy cream. I especially like to use it in my ice cream recipes. When I refer to coconut milk, I always mean the rich, full-fat variety that comes in a can. Coconut milk is frequently used in certain Asian cuisines, so you should be able to find it in the international or Asian section of your local grocery store.

COCONUT OIL

I almost exclusively use coconut oil in these recipes—mostly because I love the flavor, but also because of its health benefits. Coconut oil comes in jars in a semisolid state and can be stored in the pantry as long as the temperature doesn't exceed 75°F (24°C).

When you see a measurement for coconut oil in my recipes, it will always mean after the oil is melted—in other words, in a liquid state. If you store your coconut oil in the pantry as I do, it will already be semi-soft. To melt the oil, set the jar in a pot of warm water to gently heat it. It should melt in just a minute or two. If you're pressed for time, you can also melt it on a low-power setting in the microwave in about a minute.

COCONUT SUGAR

Coconut sugar is made from the sap of the coconut palm. Since coconut sugar is minimally processed, it's one of the few sweeteners I keep in my home. It contains trace nutrients such as potassium, zinc, calcium, and iron. It's also low on the glycemic index, which means it won't make your blood sugar spike.

EGG SUBSTITUTES

There are several ways to make substitutes for eggs. Using flax meal is my favorite method. To make the equivalent of one large egg, simply whisk together 1 tablespoon of flax meal and 3 tablespoons of warm water. You should be able to scale this up at a 3:1 ratio; I normally make a total of three "eggs" at a time. Once the flax meal and warm water are combined, put them in the refrigerator for 1 minute. The mixture will become gummy, like an egg. You can also use this method with chia seeds. I prefer flax meal, though, because it's less expensive. Another alternative is a commercial egg replacer, which is very simple to use, as well. The most popular brand that comes to mind is Ener-G-Egg Replacer. I avoid using Egg Beaters, since they're not vegan.

GOJI BERRIES

Goji berries are one of nature's superfoods. These little gems taste mildly sweet, with a slightly tart note. They're high in vitamins C and E, and recent research shows they can be a natural energy booster. Chinese-medicine practitioners often use the vibrant berries to treat blood pressure and diabetes. I add them to smoothies, oatmeal, chia pudding, and just about anything else I can. Whenever I mention goji berries in my recipes, I'm referring to the dried version.

GROUND VANILLA BEANS

Adding spices such as ground vanilla beans to foods makes them taste sweeter than they actually are, much the way adding crushed red pepper to foods makes them taste more savory. If you want to omit sugar from a recipe, adding ground vanilla beans is a great substitute. Plus, it adds an amazing flavor. Ground vanilla beans can be difficult to find in supermarkets, so I order mine online.

If you have a hard time finding ground vanilla beans, you can use a vanilla bean pod instead. Just slit the pod open and scrape the seeds out. Grind the seeds into a powder to use in the recipe, and save the pod to add flavor to sauces and milks.

You can also use vanilla extract in place of the vanilla beans. However, if you use vanilla extract in raw recipes, I suggest halving the measurement; since the food isn't cooked, you'll taste a slight flavor of alcohol.

MEDJOOL DATES

I must admit, I have a love affair with dates. I call them nature's candy because of their caramel-like sweetness. They can be used as a sugar substitute, as binding agents, and to provide a smooth texture, making them extremely versatile in baking. They're also full of fiber, so that's another benefit. One of my favorite snacks is dates stuffed with almond butter. Talk about heaven in your mouth!

There are many types of dates, but I adore the Medjool variety. They're the largest and the softest and, according to my Turkish mother-in-law, the best of them all. Having tried many different kinds of dates myself, I have to agree.

NUTS

All the nuts I use in these recipes are raw and unsalted. Since nuts can get pricey, try to stock up on them when they're on sale. I have found bulk bins to be an economical route. When you buy packaged nuts, some of your money goes to the packaging. For pricier nuts such as cashews and pecans, look for them in pieces rather than buying them whole. This alone can make a difference of a few dollars. Since you plan on blending them at home anyway, the pricier whole nuts are a waste of money.

You can save even more money by roasting and salting your nuts yourself. The Kitchen Tips on page xxvii include directions for doing so. By preparing them at home, you'll end up with nuts that are much more savory, and less expensive, than those you get from a store.

NUT SUBSTITUTES

If you or someone in your family has a nut allergy, you can still make many of these recipes by replacing the nuts with oats, sunflower seeds, flax meal, or pumpkin seeds. In recipes that call for nut milk, you can replace it with oat milk or rice milk; both are available in most grocery stores.

OATS

I use oats to give texture and sweetness to my recipes. I work almost exclusively with rolled oats, which also go by the name *old-fashioned oats*. If you're following a gluten-free diet, it's important to make sure you buy rolled oats that are labeled as such, since many oats are cut on the same machines as wheat.

OAT FLOUR

To avoid gluten in my recipes, I use oat flour. You can easily make your own gluten-free oat flour by grinding rolled oats in a blender or food processor. For 2 cups (180 g) of flour, you'll need about 3½ cups (350 g) of rolled oats.

If you can't tolerate oats, feel free to substitute gluten-free all-purpose flour in an equal substitution ratio. If you don't have a problem with wheat products, feel free to use spelt or whole wheat pastry flour, which you can also substitute at an equal ratio.

PURE MAPLE SYRUP

If I'm not using dates as a sweetener, my go-to is pure maple syrup, since it's minimally processed and has a flavor that I absolutely love. Look for brands labeled as pure maple syrup, either grade A or B. If you can afford it, I recommend going with organic as well.

RAW HONEY

A few of my recipes call for raw honey, which I use because it's less processed than other varieties and contains some trace nutrients, too. If you have allergies, local raw honey can help combat them during allergy season. If you're a vegan who doesn't use honey, feel free to substitute equal parts of pure maple syrup—you won't be disappointed either way.

SHREDDED COCONUT

Shredded coconut comes both sweetened and unsweetened. I buy the unsweetened kind, since I like to control the amount of sugar in my recipes. You can also find low-fat and full-fat varieties; I always use full-fat. Blend natural, full-fat shredded coconut in a food processor to make coconut butter, which is so melt-in-your-mouth delicious that I use it as a base for my fudge recipes.

Equipment

Before I started my blog, *My Whole Food Life*, I was a pretty typical American, with most of my meals coming from a box, jar, or can of some sort. If someone told me I could make my own almond, cashew, or Brazil nut milk or butter, I would have assumed it was too difficult. But I soon learned that could not be further from the truth—both nut milks and butters are quite simple to make.

There are some key pieces of equipment that come in handy while making them, though. Besides the most obvious utensils, such as bowls, spatulas, measuring cups, baking sheets, and so forth, a few additional appliances and tools will help simplify the task and make things a bit more organized. These items, detailed here, also have many other uses beyond making nut milk. So if you don't already own them, don't fret—you will make back what you spend on them pretty quickly, considering all the things you'll be able to make at home rather than buy.

CHEESECLOTH

A good, strong cheesecloth is essential for making nut milk and cannot be omitted from the process. I initially tried to use cheap cheesecloth, and it fell apart the first time I made milk, creating a huge mess. Make sure you buy a superfine, durable cheesecloth. Mine is ultrafine 100 percent cotton that's 9 square feet (.8 square m). The extra pennies you spend up front for high-quality cheesecloth will save you more money down the road, since it should last you a long time. I hang mine outside in the sun after using and then washing it. Not only does that help bleach the stains out naturally, but it gets rid of any smells, as well.

You can use a special nut milk bag instead, but cheesecloth works just as well.

COOKIE SCOOP

I love using a cookie scoop—it makes for nice, uniform cookies. Each one bakes evenly, since they're all the same size. Using a cookie scoop is also less messy. I used to drop cookies with two spoons, but dough would get everywhere, and the final product never looked neat. I recommend buying a high-quality cookie scoop; I got mine on Amazon after reading all the customer reviews first.

FINE-MESH STRAINER OR SIEVE

This tool is essential—making nut milk basically cannot be done without one. A fine-mesh strainer catches all the pulp after the nuts have been blended, which makes for a much smoother liquid. Mouthfeel and consistency are important when making nut milks, as too much pulp in the milk can detract from the flavor as you focus on the mush in your mouth. Since strainers and sieves come in different sizes, make sure to look for one that can sit on top of a large bowl so that you don't need to hold it while trying to pour the milk through it.

FOOD PROCESSOR

The food processor is by far the most utilized appliance in my kitchen. I use it almost every time I cook. My husband jokes that I should test food processors for the companies that make them, because I use them so frequently. They can chop nuts, grind flour, make nut butters, blend sauces, dice vegetables for soup, and so much more. If you were to ask me what one appliance you absolutely need in the kitchen, it would be this gem. It's truly a workhorse in my home. I have a 7-cup (1.75 L) Cuisinart food processor, which is large enough for my purposes. I purchased it at a reasonable price,

and I have more than made my money back using it. Most important, it cuts down on my prep time.

FUNNEL

For me, a funnel is an absolute necessity. After making a mess of my kitchen while attempting to pour nut milk from a bowl into a jar, I decided that a funnel was crucial. If you have a bowl with a pour spout on it, you may be able to skip using a funnel, but for me it's a must-have.

GLASS BOWLS

These are essential for melting chocolate. By placing a glass bowl on top of a saucepan of boiling water, you can gently melt the chocolate without burning it. This is known as the double boiler method. Glass bowls are very durable, and you needn't worry about BPA (Bisphenol A, a chemical found in many plastics) leaching into your food from them. I bought mine in a set of three, and they double as serving bowls.

GLASS JARS

I store my milk in mason jars or clear glass pitchers with a pour spout and lid. Make sure you buy jars with secure lids, because you'll need to shake the milk before every use, since some of the sediment separates from the water as the milk sits in the refrigerator. I avoid using plastic containers, as I find them more prone to leaking, and I want to stay as BPA-free as possible. My jars hold 4 cups (about 960 ml of milk, and that works well for my batches. For storing nut butters, I like to use 12-ounce (340 ml) glass mason jars, which I find to be the perfect size.

HIGH-POWERED BLENDER

Just to be clear, it is possible to make nut milks in a typical blender, but it takes much longer, since the batches have to be quite small. A high-powered blender, such as a Vitamix, Ninja, or Blendtec, can make the job easier and faster. It also does a better job of pulverizing the nuts than lower-powered blenders. It has been my experience that you can squeeze more milk out of a batch of nuts if they're blended very finely. A high-powered blender also comes in handy for making incredibly creamy nut butters. They always seem to turn out much smoother in a blender, but if chunkier butter is your thing, a food processor will suffice.

High-powered blenders can be rather expensive, but if you want to start making all of your milks at home, this will be one of the best purchases you can make and well worth the investment. Here's a little tip: with some manufacturers, if you can present a medical need for the blender, they might give you a discount. We did this for my daughter Olive, who had to use a feeding tube for the first two and a half years of her life. We used our Vitamix to blend food rather than giving her formula.

ICE CREAM MACHINE

An ice cream machine is a must for making homemade ice cream. I have a Cuisinart model and I find it very easy to use and clean. It's important to make sure the ice cream bowl has been in the freezer at least 18 hours before using it.

MEASURING CUPS AND SPOONS

Measuring cups and spoons are essential for any baking recipe. To measure dry ingredients, I like to use durable, stainless steel measuring cups, since I've had so many plastic ones break on me. For liquids, I have a glass Pyrex pitcher, which should also last a long time; plus, it has an easy-grip handle to help me keep from spilling liquids as I move it around.

MIXER

No matter how hard you try (and trust me, I have), you can never mix a batter as smoothly by hand as an electric mixer can. Whether it's a powerful stand mixer or a smaller handheld device, a mixer is a necessity for baking. I now have a KitchenAid stand mixer that I love, but I used a handheld one for years. A mixer with a whipping attachment comes in handy when making nondairy whipped cream.

MUFFIN LINERS

Muffin liners are great because they eliminate the need to grease muffin pans with oil. You can use paper liners or the reusable silicone ones, which I prefer. Muffins come out from them much more cleanly than they do with paper liners, plus there's no waste.

PARCHMENT PAPER

This is great for lining baking sheets. Unlike aluminum foil, parchment paper eliminates the need for oil to grease the pan and doesn't add a tinny aftertaste. I have found that you can often reuse the same piece of parchment paper numerous times.

PIZZA CUTTER

You're probably asking yourself, "Why would I need a pizza cutter for desserts?" Well, I love using mine to cut pieces evenly and efficiently. Sometimes running a knife through brownies or bars can pull them apart messily, which is something you don't have to worry about with a pizza cutter.

SLOW COOKER

Believe it or not, a slow cooker can be used for more than stews and chili. I've made breads, quinoa dishes, and even baked goods in my slow cooker. One of the recipes in this book, the Slow Cooker Peanut Butter Granola Bars (page 169), is made in a slow cooker, which shows that you can use appliances in ways you never thought possible.

SMALL SAUCEPAN

I call for a small saucepan in many of these recipes, since it's ideal for melting nut butter for baking. I highly recommend buying a stainless steel saucepan. Not only will it last seemingly forever, but you won't have to worry about surface pieces flaking off as you might with a Teflon pan. Plus, I find them very easy to clean after just a short soak.

SPATULAS

Spatulas are excellent tools for getting every last little bit of batter out of a bowl. I like the silicone variety, which are much more durable than the rubber ones, and they're also heat resistant. They're perfect for mixing chocolate in a double boiler.

Kitchen Tips

The following kitchen tips are meant to save you time, money, and headaches. If you follow these pointers, I promise, they'll make your life easier. I know they've helped me.

* Nuts can be very expensive, as in $10-a-pound expensive. Therefore, as I mentioned earlier, buying nuts in bulk saves a lot of money and makes a lot of cents . . . I mean, sense. The only real drawback is that you have to find an airtight container to store them in; I use glass jars for mine. Most health food stores stock bulk bins of nuts, or you can check out online sites such as Nuts.com and Vitacost.com (see page 187 for a full list of retailers). Another great tip is to buy pieces instead of whole nuts. They usually cost at least a dollar less per pound, and if you're using them to make nut butters and milks, the pieces are perfect, since they'll get blended up anyway.

* Did you know that nuts can go rancid? If you leave them out at room temperature, they will last anywhere from 1 to 12 months, depending on the type of nut. Make sure to store them in the refrigerator or freezer for longer use. If kept in the refrigerator, they can stay fresh at least 12 months, with the exception of pine nuts, which last only 4 months. If you freeze nuts, they can last up to a whopping 2 years. Of course, we all realize they'll be finished off way before then, but it's helpful to know, anyway.

* Want to save money on spices and oils? These items, especially the nicer organic brands, can quickly

become pricey. Here's a tip my Turkish mother-in-law taught me: international markets carry spices and oils at far lower prices than big-box stores. The quality is usually higher, as well. That's a hard combination to beat. If you don't have an international market near you, you can purchase spices in bulk at most health food stores. They're much cheaper that way, too. You can buy just the amount you need instead of letting that expensive, exotic spice you used once in an epic dish two years ago go stale in your pantry. I know that pain from personal experience.

* Stock up on fresh fruit when it's in season, and then freeze it to use all year long. This will save money; plus, you get to enjoy those refreshing summer berries in the middle of winter. They're great in smoothies and for baking. To freeze most fruits, you can simply lay the pieces out on a parchment-lined baking sheet and place it in the freezer. Once the fruit is frozen, put the pieces into a ziplock bag for easier storage, and then place them back in the freezer, where they should keep for up to 6 months.

* If you have hectic mornings, as I do, I suggest you make your smoothies (page 101) the night before. Once they're mixed, pour them into some ice cube trays and pop them into the freezer to re-blend in the morning. This saves a lot of time on busy days and gives you a yummy smoothie at a fraction of the prep time. You can even make a week's worth of smoothies this way. If you don't have time to clean the blender right away, pour in a drop of dishwashing liquid, fill it up halfway with water, and leave it. When you get home, blend the water for about thirty seconds and then rinse. This normally cleans the mess right up, or at least does 90 percent of the work for you.

* When you measure sticky ingredients, such as maple syrup or nut butter, make sure to brush the measuring cup with a thin layer of mild-tasting oil. This will ensure that the entire amount comes out of the measuring cup cleanly.

* Before using nuts to make milk, you'll need to soak them. This might seem as easy as putting some nuts in water and letting them sit, but

there's a bit more to it. As nutritious as nuts are, they also have natural agents built in to protect them from harmful things like early germination. These compounds, such as tannin, are great for the nut's self-defense, but they tend to be awful for our digestive system. (If you don't know what tannin is, think of it as nature's bitter-tasting pesticide that protects the nut from being gobbled up by predators.) The soaking process breaks down the agents, making them easier on our digestive system, as well as making the nuts easier to blend. It can also provide a higher nutritional value if the nuts begin to sprout in the water.

* To soak them, I fill a bowl or jar using a 2:1 water-to-nut ratio. Regular tap water is fine, and it doesn't need to be at a specific temperature. You can also add ½ teaspoon of sea salt if you like, although I usually skip that step. I've seen some sources say to soak nuts for at least 20 minutes, while others say 2 to 3 hours, and some suggest even longer than that. I normally leave mine overnight in a closed container in the refrigerator, and I recommend that you do the same. When soaking them, you'll notice the nuts begin to shed their dust and tannin. After you remove them from the soaking water, rinse them thoroughly. If you're using soaked or sprouted nuts for baking, you'll need to dry them out first, either in a dehydrator—I dry mine at about 125°F (50°C) for 10 hours—or in your oven on its lowest setting for 30 to 90 minutes, checking them often.

* When roughly chopping nuts with a knife, place a clean dish towel over the knife and the work space. The towel will keep the nuts from scattering off your cutting board. You can also use a small food processor to quickly chop them, which I highly recommend.

* Make no mistake about it—making nut milk can be a messy endeavor. Before you even start, go over the prep work first. Get all your ducks in a row by making sure each workstation is assembled and ready to go. Have the blender set up with the nuts and water. Set out a large bowl with the fine-mesh strainer on top and the cheesecloth draped over it. Lastly, have a parchment-lined

baking sheet ready and waiting to be slid into the oven to bake the nut pulp for future use. The whole process can be quite quick when you're properly organized.

* Once your nut milk is made, proper storage is key. I keep my milks in the refrigerator in a closed glass jar. Most milks last about 3 to 5 days in the refrigerator.

* As for the pulp, once it's baked and dried, it can be left out in an airtight container if you plan on using it right away. Otherwise, store it in the refrigerator in an airtight container. The pulp will last a few weeks in the refrigerator. If you plan on keeping it for more than a few weeks, you should store it in the freezer. I keep mine in a sealed ziplock bag.

* A great way to add flavor to your nut butters is to roast the nuts first, which is a very simple task. The method is the same for all nuts. Preheat the oven to 350°F (175°C). Line a baking sheet with parchment paper or a silicone liner such as a Silpat. Spread the nuts out on the baking sheet and sprinkle them with a little sea salt if you want. Roast them for 10 minutes. Stop halfway through the cooking and give the nuts a good shake to make sure they roast evenly. Wait until the nuts are completely cooled before removing them from the pan and storing them. If you choose to use roasted nuts in your nut butter recipes, you might need to add a tablespoon of mild-tasting oil to the nut butter to get a really creamy texture.

NUT MILKS

Whether you're a newbie to making milk from nuts or you're already an old pro, this chapter is for you. We have a basic recipe for nut milks for beginners, and then we'll dive into some fun flavored variations that show you how versatile nut milks can be. By the end of the chapter, making nut milk will seem so easy, you'll wonder why you ever bought it in a store. For people with nut allergies, check out the Sunflower Seed Milk recipe on page 16, which makes a great alternative to nut milks.

Almond Milk

Basic Nut Milk

MAKING NUT MILK is an easy process that's pretty consistent among varieties. The basic formula below is good for almonds, Brazil nuts, cashews, hazelnuts, and pistachios All the nuts will need to be soaked ahead of time, preferably overnight. For more on soaking, read the Kitchen Tips on page xxvii. After blending, most nut milks need to be strained through a nut milk bag or fine cheesecloth. The best advice I can give is to be prepared ahead of time. Have all of your supplies laid out where they need to be. This will keep things neat—trust me.

MAKES 4 CUPS (960 ML)

1 cup raw, unsalted nuts, whole (125 g) or chopped (70 g)

3½ to 4 cups (840 to 960 ml) water

OPTIONAL SWEETENERS:

1 teaspoon ground vanilla beans (see page xx)

½ teaspoon vanilla extract

1 Medjool date, pit removed

1 tablespoon maple syrup

1 tablespoon raw honey

1. Soak the nuts overnight. I like to use a 32-ounce (960 ml) mason jar for this, with regular tap water. It doesn't have to be a particular temperature. Place the nuts in the jar and then add enough water to cover them, plus an extra inch or two. The nuts will expand slightly during the soaking process. In the morning, drain and rinse the nuts well.

2. Add the nuts to a high-powered blender with 3½ cups (840 ml) of fresh water (see Notes on the following page). Blend for 2 minutes. I use my Vitamix, starting out at a slow speed before working my way up to a higher one.

recipe continues

3. Set a fine-mesh strainer on top of a large bowl. Place a high-quality cheesecloth on top of the strainer, or use a nut milk bag instead.

4. Pour the contents of the blender into the cheesecloth or nut milk bag. At this point, I like to walk away and let gravity do most of the work on its own. It should take about 5 minutes or so for most of the liquid to end up in the bowl.

5. Gather the cheesecloth or nut milk bag in your hands and gently squeeze it. You'll start to see a lot of liquid come out. Keep squeezing until you feel that all the liquid is gone. It can be quite the hand workout!

6. Add an optional sweetener, if desired, and then blend again for another 2 minutes.

7. Dump the excess pulp onto a parchment-lined baking sheet. It will be wet and clumpy. I use my fingers to break it up and spread it out on the baking sheet so that it dries out easily. Please don't throw it away—there are an incredible number of uses for pulp, which we'll explore later (see How to Use Nut Pulp, starting on page 57).

8. Use a funnel to pour the nut milk into a glass storage jar, and store it in the refrigerator for 3 to 4 days, or in the freezer for up to 2 months.

NOTES

* If you decide to add a sweetener or two to this recipe, start with ground vanilla beans, which make things taste sweeter without raising the actual sugar content. Be sure to strain the milk *before* adding the sweetener. If you add the sweetener too early in the process, some of it will get caught in the cheesecloth, especially dates. I add the dates once I have strained the mixture, and then I blend everything again for another 2 minutes to make sure the ingredients are completely mixed. Note that if you use vanilla extract, you might be able to slightly taste the alcohol, since this recipe isn't cooked.

* As you start playing around with the types of nuts you use, you'll notice that not all of them need to be strained after they're blended. Some, such as cashews and pistachios, create a very fine powder that goes straight through the

cheesecloth. For those, I simply blend, pour, chill, and serve.

* Don't be shocked when you take your milk out of the refrigerator and find that it's separated. Just give it a good shake to mix it up again. Homemade nut milk doesn't have added thickeners, emulsifiers, or stabilizers to keep the mixture homogeneous.

* If you don't have a high-powered blender, you can use a regular blender. You'll just need to make the milk in smaller batches—about ½ cup (65 g) of nuts to 1¾ cups (420 ml) of water at a time.

* Most nut milks will last 3 to 4 days in the refrigerator, which should be plenty of time if you use them regularly in coffee, cereal, and recipes. The somewhat short life span is why I don't make it in large batches. Store-bought milks tend to last longer because they have added preservatives.

PREP TIME: About 15 minutes (not including the overnight soak), plus 2 hours if drying the pulp for later use (see page 57)

Chocolate Cashew Milk

IT SEEMS THAT every kid loves chocolate milk, and what adult doesn't reminisce about drinking the thick, sweet stuff? Well, here's a healthier, grown-up version for you. It's a luxurious milk that makes an amazing hot chocolate on cold, snowy days or works wonderfully as an after-dinner drink. The recipe is easy, as well: simply blend, pour, and enjoy— no straining required. Chocolate isn't the only delicious, satisfying flavor you can add to your nut milks! The next few recipes will show you just how versatile nuts can be.

MAKES 4 CUPS (960 ML)

1 cup (130 g) raw, unsalted cashews, soaked overnight (see page xxix)

3½ cups (840 ml) water

One 3.5-ounce (100 g) dark chocolate bar or ½ cup (80 g) chocolate chips

1 tablespoon unsweetened cocoa powder

1 teaspoon cinnamon

2 Medjool dates, pits removed

1. Drain and rinse the cashews.

2. Chop the chocolate bar roughly There's no need to chop it finely, since you'll be putting it into the blender.

3. Add all the ingredients to a high-powered blender and blend until smooth, about 2 to 3 minutes.

4. Serve the milk immediately, or store it in the refrigerator for later use. It will keep for 3 to 4 days.

NOTE

You can strain the milk if you like, but it isn't really necessary with cashew

recipe continues

milk, since the nuts are naturally soft and blend easily.

Variations

* You can replace the Medjool dates with 2 teaspoons of raw honey or pure maple syrup if you prefer. I just like the way the dates sweeten the milk.

* A fun idea is to pour the chocolate cashew milk into freezer-pop molds. They will need at least 6 hours to firm up in the freezer, but when they do, you'll have some dairy-free "Fudgsicles," which make a delightful treat on a hot day.

PREP TIME: 10 minutes (not including the overnight soak)

Strawberry Brazil Nut Milk

BRAZIL NUTS PRODUCE extremely thick, velvety milk that could be considered the full-fat version of the nut milk world. I regularly drink it on its own, but my kids love flavored milk, so I created this recipe with them in mind. I typically use strawberries, as the recipe suggests, but it works well with any berry, even frozen ones if fresh aren't available because of the season or location. If you choose to use frozen berries, just make sure they're thawed before starting the recipe.

MAKES 1½ CUPS (360 ML)

1 cup (240 ml) Brazil nut milk
(see Basic Nut Milk recipe, page 3)

1 cup (125 g) sliced strawberries
(fresh, or frozen and thawed)

1 teaspoon ground vanilla beans
(see page xx)

1. Combine all the ingredients in a blender and mix for 1 to 2 minutes at high speed. A high-powered blender is ideal; a regular blender or Magic Bullet will also do the job, although you might have to blend the ingredients a little longer.

2. You can drink the strawberry milk as is or, if desired, pour it through a fine-mesh strainer to remove the pulp. Either way works—it depends on your preference.

3. Serve the milk immediately, or store it in the refrigerator for later use. It will keep for up to 3 days.

NOTES

* If you're using tart strawberries, you can add a sweetener. I recommend 1 Medjool date or 2 teaspoons of pure maple syrup.
* You can substitute an equal quantity of vanilla extract for the vanilla beans, but you might be able to slightly taste the alcohol if you do, since this recipe isn't cooked.

PREP TIME: 5 minutes (not including the overnight soak)

Strawberry Brazil Nut Milk,
page 9

Vanilla Hazelnut Milk,
page 12

Vanilla Hazelnut Milk

I'VE NEVER MET anyone who doesn't love hazelnuts (also known as filberts). They make an excellent butter, which is magnificent when mixed with chocolate, as in my Chocolate Hazelnut Spread (page 34). Here's a way to enjoy them as a milk. This drink will remind you why hazelnuts are universally adored. It has a luxurious flavor that keeps me coming back for more. I even put it in my morning coffee as a creamer. Plus the pulp is like a gift that keeps on giving—try it in the Grain-Free Energy Bites (page 65) or Protein-Packed Snack Balls (page 67). I can't say enough about the virtues of this nut.

MAKES 4 CUPS (960 ML)

1 cup (135 g) raw, unsalted hazelnuts, soaked overnight (see page xxix)

3½ cups (840 ml) water

1 teaspoon ground vanilla beans (see page xx)

1. Drain and rinse the hazelnuts.
2. Add the nuts and water to a high-powered blender (see Notes on page xxv if you don't have one of these), and blend until smooth, about 2 to 3 minutes.
3. Set a fine-mesh strainer on top of a large bowl. Place a high-quality cheesecloth on top of the strainer, or use a nut milk bag instead.
4. Slowly pour the milk into the cheese-cloth or nut milk bag, making sure not to overfill the container. You will need to do this in batches to avoid making a mess.

5. Gather the cheesecloth or nut milk bag in your hands, and gently squeeze it. Keep squeezing until you feel that all the liquid is gone.

6. Dump the leftover pulp onto a parchment-lined baking sheet (see How to Use Nut Pulp on page 57).

7. Repeat these steps until all the milk is extracted.

8. Pour the milk back into the blender, and add the vanilla and a sweetener if you choose (see Notes below). Briefly blend.

9. Serve the milk immediately, or store it in the refrigerator for later use. It will keep for up to 4 days.

NOTES

† You can substitute vanilla extract for the vanilla beans, but you might be able to slightly taste the alcohol if you do. since this recipe isn't cooked.

✳ If you want a sweeter milk, try blending in 1 to 2 Medjool dates (my personal favorite) or 2 teaspoons of maple syrup. Adding stevia is another possibility, but it can leave a slightly bitter aftertaste, so I don't recommend it. However, if you're used to the taste of stevia, feel free to mix in 2 to 3 drops.

PREP TIME: About 15 minutes (not including the overnight soak)

Spiced Pistachio Milk

PISTACHIO MILK IS one of the easiest nut milks to make. There's no straining necessary, and it makes a super-creamy milk that tastes magnificent in your morning coffee. To make this recipe even better, I've added some spices that pair well with its rich texture. This is one drink you'll want to make over and over again. I advise you to buy unsalted, shelled pistachios. Purchasing unshelled pistachios is fine, but it makes for a long and frustrating preparation.

MAKES 6 CUPS (1.4 L)

1 cup (125 g) raw, unsalted pistachios, soaked overnight (see page xxix)

3½ cups (840 ml) water

1 teaspoon cinnamon

¼ teaspoon ground ginger

¼ teaspoon ground nutmeg

2 Medjool dates, pits removed

1. Drain and rinse the pistachios.

2. Add the pistachios, water, cinnamon, ginger, and nutmeg to a high-powered blender (see page xxv if you don't have one of these). If you have a variable-speed blender, start on a low setting and work your way up to high over a period of 1 to 2 minutes. If you don't have a variable-speed blender, simply mix on high for 1 to 2 minutes.

3. Set a fine-mesh strainer on top of a large bowl, and slowly pour the mixture through the strainer. There really shouldn't be much to strain; I don't use a cheesecloth at all for this recipe.

4. Pour the milk back into the blender and add the dates. Blend for 2 minutes to make sure the dates are completely ground up.

5. Serve the milk immediately, or store it in the refrigerator for later use. It will keep for 3 to 4 days

PREP TIME: About 15 minutes (not including the overnight soak)

Sunflower Seed Milk

I KNOW SUNFLOWER seeds aren't nuts, but I wanted to include them, since so many people suffer from nut allergies these days. It may seem unbelievable, but you can actually make milk from these tiny seeds. You can create sunflower butter, too—check out the Sunflower Seed Butter recipe on page 55. The process for making Sunflower Seed Milk is very simple and really no different than making nut milk.

MAKES 3 CUPS (720 ML)

1 cup (140 g) raw, unsalted sunflower seeds (soaked overnight, see page xxix)

4 cups (960 ml) water

1. Drain and rinse the sunflower seeds.
2. Place the seeds in a blender with 4 cups (960 ml) of fresh water. Blend on high for 1 to 2 minutes.
3. Set a fine-mesh strainer on top of a large bowl. Place a high-quality cheesecloth on top of the strainer.
4. Slowly pour the milk into the cheesecloth, making sure not to put too much in at once. You will need to do this in batches to avoid making a mess.
5. Gather the cheesecloth in your hands, and gently squeeze it. Keep squeezing until you feel that all the liquid is gone.
6. Dump the leftover pulp onto a parchment-lined baking sheet (see How to Use Nut Pulp on page 57).

7. Repeat these steps until all the milk is extracted.
8. Place a funnel on top of the storage container for your milk and pour in the liquid. I like to use 32-ounce (960 ml) glass mason jars, which fit this recipe perfectly.
9. Serve the milk immediately, or store it in the refrigerator for later use. It will keep for 3 to 4 days

NOTES

* If you've ever tried rice milk, you know that it has a thin texture, especially compared to nut milk. Sunflower Seed Milk is very similar in that aspect. If you want it slightly thicker, you can add 2 teaspoons of arrowroot to the milk after you pour it into the storage container. Simply mix well.
* You can add a tablespoon of honey or pure maple syrup if you like your milk a little sweet. Add the sweetener after you strain the mixture, and then blend again for another minute to make sure everything is completely mixed.

PREP TIME: About 20 minutes (not including the overnight soak)

Sunflower Seed Milk,
page 16

Hot Chocolate Cashew Milk,
page 20

Hot Chocolate Cashew Milk

IN THE DEAD of winter we can all go for a little coziness, and there's something delightfully comforting about warm milk. We may think of nut milk as a cold refreshment, but it can be used to make some delicious hot drinks, too. Cashew milk is incredibly creamy by nature, making it the perfect base for hot chocolate, and, luckily, this recipe is oh-so-easy to make. I add a little cinnamon to spice it up, and nutmeg can be a nice touch as well. If you like an extra bit of heat, try including a pinch of cayenne. See the Bonus Recipe for Coconut Whipped Cream on the following page to make this an even more deluxe treat..

MAKES TWO 1-CUP (240 ML) SERVINGS

2 cups (480 ml) cashew milk (see Basic Nut Milk recipe, page 3)

Heaping ¼ cup (40 g) dark chocolate chips

3 tablespoons unsweetened cocoa powder

½ teaspoon cinnamon

2 tablespoons pure maple syrup, optional

1. Mix all the ingredients in a saucepan over medium heat. You can add maple syrup if you like your drinks a little sweeter, but personally I don't think it needs it.

2. Stir until all the ingredients are mixed and the chocolate chips have melted, 5 to 7 minutes. Serve immediately.

Variations

* Try adding a shot of espresso to make this a mocha drink.
* If you have a milk frother, you can froth a bit of extra nut milk on top to create a homemade cappuccino.

PREP TIME: About 10 minutes, not including Coconut Whipped Cream

BONUS RECIPE

Coconut Whipped Cream

If you want a dollop of whipped cream on top of your hot chocolate, you can easily make it with coconut milk. All you need is one 14-ounce (400 ml) can of full-fat coconut milk and 1 to 2 teaspoons of pure maple syrup.

Refrigerate the unopened can of coconut milk overnight. When you open it the next morning, you'll see that the fatty part of the coconut milk has separated from the water. That fatty part makes the most wonderful, dairy-free whipped cream!

Spoon out the fatty part of the coconut milk into a small mixing bowl. You can freeze the leftover coconut water in ice cube trays to add to smoothies (see page 101). Using the whipping attachment on your mixer, whip the coconut fat into a cream. This will take 2 to 3 minutes on high speed. The result should resemble a whipped cream made from heavy dairy cream. I highly recommend using the whipped cream right away, since it will harden if you refrigerate it.

Spiced Chai Milk

SERVED WARM AND with a little touch of spice, this drink is perfect for relaxing after a busy day. It's also delicious chilled and used as a coffee creamer.

MAKES 1 CUP (240 ML)

1 cup (240 ml) nut milk of choice (see Basic Nut Milk recipe, page 3)

1 teaspoon pure maple syrup

½ teaspoon cinnamon

½ teaspoon ground vanilla beans (see page xx)

¼ teaspoon ground nutmeg

1. Place all the ingredients in a blender or Magic Bullet and blend for 1 to 2 minutes on high, until the ingredients are well mixed.

2. Pour the mixture into a small saucepan and place over medium heat, stirring every few minutes until it reaches the temperature you desire. Make sure to watch it closely; it can quickly bubble over if you're not careful.

3. Serve the milk immediately, or refrigerate it for up to 4 days for use as a coffee creamer.

NOTE

I highly recommend using almond milk or Brazil nut milk in this recipe. Both have creamy textures that work well with these flavors.

PREP TIME: 5 to 7 minutes

NUT BUTTERS

Once you realize how easy nut butters are to make, you'll probably laugh at yourself for not trying it sooner. You'll also never buy them from a supermarket again. The preparation doesn't take long, the butter lasts quite a while if properly stored, and it tastes more flavorful than commercial versions do. If you keep your nut butter in the fridge, it can last for several months, although we usually go through it much more quickly than that in our house. You can make butter from just about any nut, with each variety offering its own unique, finger-licking-good flavor. The following recipes will show you that homemade nut butter soars way beyond the standard peanut butter.

Basic Nut Butter

THE CONCEPT BEHIND making nut butters is pretty simple: just blend the nuts until they reach the creaminess you desire. The process is the same for all nuts. You should make nut butter in small batches to get the best results and to avoid burning out your blender or food processor. If you prefer it a bit chunky, as I do, a food processor works well, or you can use a blender for a finer, smoother consistency. I have made nut butter in a food processor, a Vitamix, and my Blendtec using the Twister Jar (see Notes on the following page).

MAKES ½ CUP (125 G)

1 cup (125 g) nuts (see Notes on the following page)

1. Grind the nuts in a food processor or a high-powered blender. The food processor requires a little more time, but you won't have to scrape down the sides as often, and it's easier to clean. Both work equally well; you simply need to decide which one is better for you.

2. Blend until the butter is smooth, scraping down the sides of the canister periodically. The time this takes depends on the nuts. Brazil nuts, macadamias, peanuts, pecans, and walnuts all take about 5 minutes. Almonds, hazelnuts, pistachios, and sunflower seeds can take up to 20 minutes. For those that take longer, I suggest pausing the blending process every 5 minutes to give the machine a break and allow the nuts to release some of their oils.

3. Transfer the butter to an airtight container for storage. I store my nut butter on the counter and it will keep for a few weeks, but it's usually gobbled up before then! If you plan on saving it longer than 2 weeks, I recommend refrigerating it. It can last up to 4 months in the refrigerator, since the cold

temperature helps keep the oils from going rancid.

NOTES

* I typically make my nut butters with raw, unsalted nuts. You can use roasted nuts (see page xxx for directions), but you might need to add at least 1½ teaspoons of a mild-tasting oil to get a smooth, buttery consistency.
* Please make sure the nuts are fresh. If they're old, they will not create a smooth consistency.
* If you choose to use the Blendtec Twister Jar, I recommend making 1 cup (250 g) of nut butter at a time. Even if you don't have a powerful food processor or blender, you can make nut butter using a smaller appliance like a Magic Bullet. If you go that route, cut the recipe in half to ½ cup (65 g) of nuts.

Variations

If you want to add flavorings such as oil, sea salt, or sweetener, do so after you have made the nut butter so that you'll know what your base consistency and flavor is. Some suggestions are ½ teaspoon of sea salt; 1 teaspoon of sweetener, such as pure maple syrup or raw honey; or ½ to 1 tablespoon of oil (I like to use coconut, grape seed, or olive).

PREP TIME: 5 to 20 minutes, depending on the type of nut you use

Classic Peanut Butter

THIS IS THE classic nut butter recipe, making it a great starting point. You can use any type of peanuts you desire: raw, roasted, salted, or unsalted. They're all delicious. I prefer using roasted, unsalted peanuts for this butter, because it allows me to control the salt content, and I love that great roasted flavor. If you use roasted peanuts, remember to add a little oil to keep the peanut butter moist throughout the process. This recipe works perfectly for the Peanut Butter Cup Granola (page 85) or Peanut Butter Chocolate Chip Donuts (page 89).

MAKES 1 CUP (250 G)

2 cups (280 g) peanuts, roasted (see page xxx) or raw

½ teaspoon sea salt

1 to 2 tablespoons mild-tasting oil, if using roasted peanuts

1. Grind the peanuts and sea salt in a food processor or high-powered blender until creamy, 5 to 10 minutes. If you're using a blender, I recommend starting on a low speed and then working your way up to high. You might need to stop several times to scrape down the sides.

2. Transfer the peanut butter to an airtight container for storage. It should keep at room temperature for up to 2 weeks, or up to 4 months in the refrigerator.

PREP TIME: 5 to 10 minutes

Salted Honey Cashew Butter

THE RICH, SMOOTH taste of cashew butter makes it one of the most special nut butters, in my opinion. Sweet and salty, always a winning combination, join forces perfectly in this extra-luxurious salted honey cashew butter. You might be tempted to eat it straight from the jar—I find that bread just gets in the way. It's also a perfect filling for truffles (page 129).

MAKES ½ CUP (160 G)

1 cup (130 g) raw cashews

1 tablespoon raw honey or pure maple syrup

½ teaspoon sea salt (see Note below)

1. Grind the cashews in a food processor or high-powered blender for 5 to 10 minutes, stopping often to scrape down the sides. Start at a low speed and slowly work your way up to high.

2. Add the honey and sea salt and continue to blend until smooth. This should require only a few more minutes.

3. Transfer the butter to an airtight glass storage container. It should keep at room temperature for up to 2 weeks, or up to 4 months in the refrigerator.

NOTE

If you buy salted cashews, omit the salt in this recipe.

PREP TIME: 8 to 12 minutes

Rich and Creamy Pistachio Butter

I DON'T KNOW about you, but a bag of pistachios never lasts long in my house, even with the hassle of shelling them. There's just something about their smooth texture that makes them so appealing. Add some salt and you have yourself a handy snack! Throw them in a blender and you get a velvety butter that you can use in cookies, ice cream (see page 179), truffles (see page 129), and other treats. I especially love using pistachios in truffles, since their pretty green hue contrasts beautifully against the chocolate, making them ideal for the holidays.

MAKES ½ CUP (140 G)

1 cup (125 g) raw, unsalted pistachios
½ teaspoon sea salt
1 teaspoon pure maple syrup

1. Grind the nuts and the sea salt in a food processor or high-powered blender on high speed for 10 to 15 minutes. You might need to scrape down the sides of the blender or food processor several times.
2. When the mixture is almost smooth, add the maple syrup, and blend for another 2 minutes.
3. Transfer the butter to an airtight glass container for storage. It should keep at room temperature for up to 2 weeks, or up to 4 months in the refrigerator.

NOTE

This pistachio butter is also wonderful in place of the pecan butter in Pecan Caramel Overnight Oats (page 94). Delicious!

PREP TIME: 10 to 15 minutes

Chocolate Hazelnut Spread

HAZELNUTS ARE ONE of my favorite nuts to use in the kitchen, perhaps because my mother was German. Since many German desserts and candies contain hazelnuts, recipes like this one take me back to my childhood. This spread can be enjoyed in so many different ways. Smear it on toast, waffles, crepes, or pancakes, or add a spoonful to Pecan Caramel Overnight Oats (page 94). It's also wonderful in Banana Muffins with Chocolate Hazelnut Filling (page 83). Unlike the popular store-bought chocolate hazelnut spread, this one does not contain processed sugar or soy. Try this easy recipe and you'll never have the urge to purchase the commercial brand again.

MAKES 1½ CUPS (360 G)

2 cups (240 g) raw, unsalted hazelnuts

1 cup (240 ml) almond milk (see Basic Nut Milk recipe, page 3)

⅓ cup (40 g) unsweetened cocoa powder

3 tablespoons pure maple syrup or raw honey

2 teaspoons ground vanilla beans (see page xx)

1. You can remove the hazelnut skins or leave them on; I've done it both ways. If you decide to remove the skins, you'll need to roast the nuts first (see page xxx for directions).

2. Wait until the hazelnuts are completely cooled before attempting to remove the skins; otherwise you'll burn your hands. It should take about 5 minutes for the hazelnuts to cool down enough to handle. Once cooled, rub them between your palms to remove the skins.

3. Grind the hazelnuts in a blender until they have a coarse consistency, about 1 minute. I highly recommend using a high-powered blender to get a smoother texture. You can use a food processor, but you might need to grind the nuts for about 2 minutes longer and a slight graininess may remain. It will still taste divine; it

will just have a different texture. I have tested this recipe with both appliances and find that the hazelnut spread made in the blender most closely resembles the store-bought variety.

4. Add the almond milk, cocoa powder, maple syrup, and vanilla. Blend until smooth, about 2 minutes.

5. Because this recipe contains almond milk, it needs to be stored in the refrigerator. It should last 7 to 10 days.

NOTE

You can substitute 1 teaspoon of vanilla extract for the ground vanilla beans, but you might be able to slightly taste the alcohol if you do, since this recipe isn't cooked.

PREP TIME: 5 to 7 minutes (longer if removing the skins first)

Chocolate Hazelnut Spread,
page 34

Chocolate Peanut Butter Spread,
page 38

Chocolate Peanut Butter Spread

SINCE THE BEGINNING of their mutual existence, chocolate and peanut butter have been paired together. Some of the most popular desserts in Western culture today are based on this wonderful combination, be it a sumptuous mousse at an expensive restaurant or a common candy bar impulsively purchased at the checkout line in a grocery store. They're the perfect match, with the saltiness of the peanuts and the melt-in-your-mouth sweetness of the chocolate too good to pass up. I simply had to include this recipe in the book. This spread is great on toast, waffles, or ice cream, or you can just eat it by the spoonful!

MAKES 1 CUP (300 G)

1½ cups (210 g) raw peanuts (see Notes on the following page)

1 cup (160 g) dark chocolate chips

1¾ cups (420 ml) almond milk (see Basic Nut Milk recipe, page 3)

2 tablespoons pure maple syrup

1. Grind the peanuts in a food processor or high-powered blender on high speed until they have a coarse consistency, 1 to 2 minutes.

2. Add the chocolate chips and continue to pulse for a few more minutes to mix.

3. Add the almond milk and maple syrup and blend for another 3 minutes, or until the spread reaches the consistency you desire.

4. Transfer the spread to a glass jar for storage. Because this recipe contains almond milk, it needs to be stored in the refrigerator, where it should last for up to 2 weeks.

NOTES

* You can make this with salted or unsalted peanuts; I use unsalted. If you go with unsalted peanuts and would still like a salty element, I suggest adding ½ teaspoon of sea salt. You can mix it in at the same time as the almond milk and maple syrup.

* I keep this spread in 12-ounce (340 ml), wide-mouth glass mason jars, which fit the recipe yield perfectly.

* This spread will firm up after being in the fridge. Before using, let it sit at room temperature for about 30 minutes, or heat it in a microwave at half power for 1 minute.

PREP TIME: 5 to 7 minutes

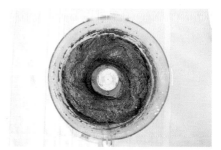

Maple Vanilla Almond Butter

HAVING GROWN UP in the Northeast, I can attest to the magic of anything maple, from maple butter to maple syrup. The natural sweetener makes everything better, and it pairs perfectly with vanilla, which really stands out in this flavorful spread. Adding ground vanilla beans to a dish can make it taste sweeter than it really is, which makes using vanilla a terrific way to cut sugar consumption while still indulging. I promise this classic combination will have you coming back for more.

MAKES ¾ CUP (175 G)

1 cup (125 g) raw, unsalted almonds

2 tablespoons pure maple syrup

1 teaspoon ground vanilla beans (see page xx)

½ teaspoon sea salt

1. Grind the almonds in a food processor or a high-powered blender on high speed (see Notes below). Pause every few minutes to give the almonds time to release their oils.
2. Once the almonds look moist, after 10 to 15 minutes, add the remaining ingredients and blend until smooth.
3. Transfer the butter to an airtight glass container for storage. It should keep at room temperature for up to 2 weeks, or up to 4 months in the refrigerator.

NOTES

* You can substitute vanilla extract for the vanilla beans, cutting the amount down to ½ teaspoon, but you might be able to slightly taste the alcohol if you do, since this recipe isn't cooked.
* The time it takes to make almond butter varies depending on the type of equipment you use; it typically takes about 15 to 25 minutes. A high-powered blender will be faster than a food processor. Both have

recipe continues

their pros and cons. While the food processor might take longer, the cleanup is much easier and the sides don't need to be scraped as often. A blender is quicker, but it requires more scraping and a more difficult cleanup. Either way, this recipe is worth the time and effort.

PREP TIME: 15 to 25 minutes

Apple Donuts and Sandwiches

Here's a fun serving suggestion for this Maple Vanilla Almond Butter: use it in apple donuts and apple sandwiches. I enjoy making these simple, healthy snacks with my daughters, who love them! If your child is allergic to nuts or attends a nut-free school, you can substitute Sunflower Seed Butter (page 55) for the almond butter. Here's how you make them:

Take an apple of your choice (I like Honeycrisp) and slice it into ¼-inch-thick circles. If you have very young children, you can peel the apple before slicing it. What you end up with are about 6 apple circles with a little core in the middle of each one. Use a small circular cookie cutter or a knife to cut the core out of each apple slice.

To make donuts, simply spread the nut butter on top of each slice, and then give the kids some toppings to add. We like to use shredded, unsweetened coconut, raw sunflower seeds, dried fruit, chopped nuts, or cacao nibs.

If you want apple sandwiches, just stack two slices of apple on top of each other with the nut butter in the middle. Apple sandwiches make excellent snacks for school. If you want to keep your apples from browning in the lunch box, simply squeeze a tiny drop of lemon juice onto each slice.

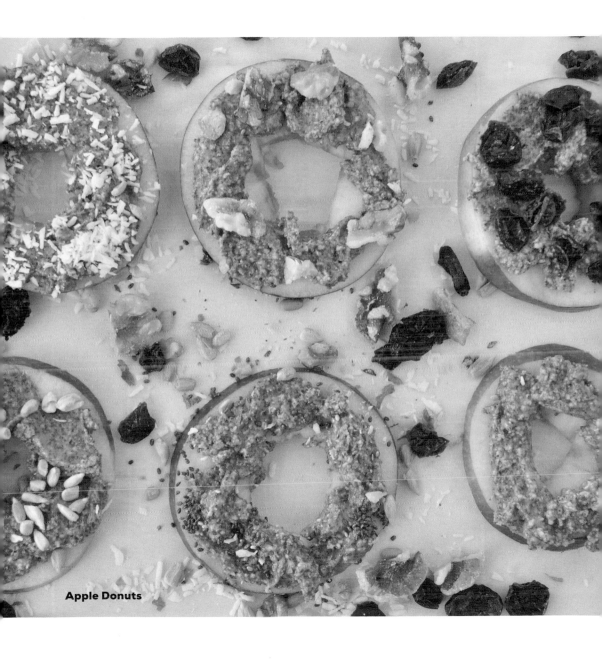

Apple Donuts

Cinnamon Pecan Butter

PECANS HAVE A natural sweetness that I'm incredibly fond of, and they make an ideal nut butter. I sometimes use pecan butter as the base in my truffles (see page 129), since it's so rich in flavor without any extra sugar. When you add cinnamon to the mix, it takes the taste to a whole new level. I'm sure this will become a staple in your house as it has in mine. Try using it in place of the Chocolate Hazelnut Spread in my Banana Muffins (page 83).

MAKES ½ CUP (160 G)

1½ cups (150 g) raw, unsalted pecans
1 teaspoon cinnamon
½ teaspoon sea salt

1. Combine all the ingredients in a food processor or high-powered blender. Blend on high speed until the mixture reaches the consistency you desire. If you use a blender, this should take only about 2 minutes; a food processor will need 5 to 7 minutes.

2. Transfer the butter to an airtight glass container for storage. It should keep at room temperature for up to 2 weeks, or up to 4 months in the refrigerator.

NOTE

If you decide to add a sweetener, mix it in when the butter looks almost ready. I recommend using 1 teaspoon of pure maple syrup or 1 teaspoon of raw honey.

PREP TIME: 5 to 10 minutes

Maple Cinnamon Macadamia Spread

THIS SPICE-FILLED NUT butter is sure to comfort you on a cold day. Sweet and buttery, bursting with hints of cinnamon and nutmeg, it makes a wonderful dip for fruit or cookies, or you can give new life to your morning toast by using it instead of butter or jam.

MAKES 1¼ CUP (330 G)

2 cups (280 g) raw, unsalted macadamia nuts

2 tablespoons pure maple syrup

1 teaspoon cinnamon

1 teaspoon sea salt

¼ teaspoon ground nutmeg

1. Grind the nuts in a food processor or high-powered blender on high speed for 1 to 2 minutes.

2. Add the remaining ingredients and continue to blend until the mixture is smooth. This should take less than 5 minutes. Scrape down the sides of the blender as needed.

3. Transfer the butter to an airtight glass container for storage. It should keep at room temperature for up to 2 weeks, or up to 4 months in the refrigerator.

NOTES

* I find that this spread tastes even better warm, so keep that in mind when serving it. I warm the spread by sticking the jar in a bowl of hot

water for a few minutes, or you can heat it gently in a microwave on half power for no longer than 20 seconds.

* I've discovered that a 4-ounce (120 ml) mason jar fits this recipe perfectly.

Variation

Apples and nuts go perfectly together, so if you want to kick things up a notch, add ¼ cup (60 ml) of unsweetened applesauce (see page xviii). This mixture tastes great on toast or even swirled into a cup of plain yogurt.

PREP TIME: 7 to 10 minutes

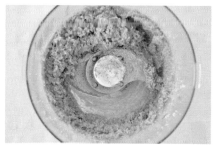

Maple Cinnamon
Macadamia Spread, page 46

Chunky Banana Walnut Spread, page 50

Chunky Banana Walnut Spread

THIS IS NOT your mama's nut butter—this stuff is over-the-top awesome, with a deep and unending flavor. The richness of the walnut butter mixed with the sweetness of the ripe banana tastes amazing together in this epic spread. I highly suggest spreading some on top of pancakes or waffles; I promise you'll love it.

MAKES 1 CUP (330 G)

2 cups (200 g) raw, unsalted walnuts, plus an extra handful to mix in for an added crunch

1 large very ripe banana

1 to 1½ teaspoons cinnamon

1. Grind the walnuts in a food processor or high-powered blender on high speed for 1 to 2 minutes, until they begin to clump together slightly.

2. Add the banana and cinnamon and blend until smooth, another 2 minutes. Gently fold in the extra walnuts for an additional crunch, or you can omit them and leave it smooth.

3. Transfer the butter to an airtight glass container for storage. It should keep in the refrigerator for up to 1 week.

NOTE

After this spread has been refrigerated for a while it will harden a bit, so you'll need to pull it out about 30 minutes before using it. You can also set the jar in a bowl of warm water to soften it.

PREP TIME: About 5 minutes

Banana Walnut Freezer Fudge

You can make a heavenly freezer fudge using the basic ingredients in this recipe. Take 2 cups (200 g) of walnuts, 1 mashed banana, and 1 tablespoon of pure maple syrup, and mix them together in a food processor or blender on high speed. Scoop the mixture into the lined cups of a standard muffin pan and place the pan in the freezer. After about 4 hours, you'll have a decadent fudge with very little added sugar. This recipe makes 10 to 12 pieces of fudge, depending on how large you cut them.

Salted "Caramel" Brazil Nut Butter

BRAZIL NUT BUTTER is one of the quickest nut butters you can make. If you have a high-powered blender, you should be able to do it in about 2 minutes. The sweet and salty combo of this recipe makes it highly addictive. The Medjool dates provide a caramel-like taste and texture in a much healthier way than the actual sugary stuff, and the sea salt enhances all of the flavors. You can spread this nut butter on toast or simply eat it with a spoon. To use it in a fun, creative way, try melting it over some ice cream.

MAKES 1½ CUPS (360 G)

2½ cups (360 g) raw, unsalted Brazil nuts

5 Medjool dates, pits removed

1½ teaspoons sea salt

1. Grind the Brazil nuts in a high-powered blender or food processor on high speed until completely crumbled, 2 to 4 minutes.
2. Add the dates and sea salt, then continue to blend until the mixture is smooth, another 1 to 2 minutes.
3. Transfer the butter to an airtight glass storage container. It should keep at room temperature for up to 1 week, or up to 3 weeks in the refrigerator.

NOTE

If you store this butter in the fridge, it might harden a little. To soften it back up, simply stick the jar in a bowl of very warm water for about 2 minutes. You can also gently heat it in a microwave at half power for 30 seconds, which should loosen it up.

PREP TIME: 5 to 7 minutes

Sunflower Seed Butter

TECHNICALLY SUNFLOWER SEEDS are not nuts. However, I felt the need to include them in this book, since so many people suffer from nut allergies these days, and sunflower seeds can make a tasty spread. If you or someone you know is allergic to nuts, sunflower seeds are a great alternative. This butter is very easy to make, although it does require some patience.

MAKES 1 CUP (300 G)

2 cups (280 g) raw, unsalted sunflower seeds

2 tablespoons olive oil

½ teaspoon sea salt

1. Grind the sunflower seeds in a food processor or a high-powered blender for 2 to 3 minutes on high. Stop and give the seeds a few minutes to release some of their natural oils.

2. Start processing the seeds again, scraping down the sides often. Pause every few minutes to give the blender a rest and to allow the seeds to release more oils.

3. After about 10 minutes, the mixture will start to get moist and clump together. Add the olive oil and sea salt. Continue to process until it forms a spread. Making

recipe continues

Sunflower Seed Butter takes much longer than nut butter, usually 20 to 25 minutes.

4. Transfer the butter to an airtight glass container for storage. It should keep at room temperature or in the refrigerator for 2 to 3 weeks.

NOTES

If you have a high-powered blender such as a Vitamix, Ninja, or Blendtec, this process will be much faster, although you'll probably have to scrape down the sides more often. I used my Blendtec with the Twister Jar attachment, which cuts down on the time a bit.

PREP TIME: About 25 minutes

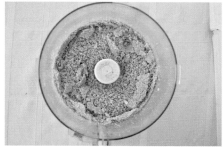

How to Use Nut Pulp

After making nut milks, you'll be left with pulp. The good news? This pulp is not trash and has so many excellent uses. The bad news? There is none. Similar to nut meal or nut flour, nut pulp is commonly utilized in gluten-free baking. It can be substituted in recipes that call for nut meals or flours, mixed into smoothies or oatmeal for additional protein and fiber, added to energy bites or other raw snacks in place of nut meals or flours, or sprinkled onto applesauce or yogurt as a crunchy topping—just use your imagination! I've included some recipes here that demonstrate how diverse and useful nut pulp can be.

Basic Nut Pulp

NO COMPONENTS OF the "milking" process need wind up in the garbage or compost heap—nut pulp has an endless number of uses! Below is my recipe for creating nut pulp. Keep in mind that since the pulp is quite moist right after the milking process, it will need to be dried out, either in an oven or a food dehydrator (see Note on the following page). I usually use the oven, since it's a bit quicker.

1. Preheat the oven to 225°F (110°C). Spread the pulp out evenly on a parchment-lined baking sheet.
2. Bake it in the oven for about 2 hours, until no moisture remains. Take it out of the oven every 30 minutes and try to break up the large clumps by gently mashing them with a fork. This helps to dry out the pulp more quickly. If the pulp isn't completely dry at the end of 2 hours, continue cooking a little longer, checking its progress often.
3. The dried nut pulp will still be a little clumpy. To break it apart completely, let the pulp cool in the pan and then blend it into a fine powder in the blender.

4. Use a funnel to pour it into a glass storage jar and store it in the refrigerator for 3 to 4 days, or in the freezer for up to 2 months.

NOTE

If you're drying the pulp in a dehydrator, set the temperature to 135°F (57°C) and cook it for 4 to 6 hours. Check on it every hour to break up the clumps.

PREP AND BAKE TIME: 2 to 3 hours

Grain-Free Peanut Butter Banana Pancakes

GRAIN-FREE BAKING HAS many benefits, one being that the food is gluten-free. Although not everyone is allergic to gluten, it seems that more and more people are trying to avoid it. Removing the grains also makes a dish low-carb. This means it's perfect for diabetics and those who follow a paleo diet. The texture of grain-free pancakes isn't the same as that of traditional pancakes, so don't fret if they come out slightly different from what you're used to.

MAKES TEN 4-INCH (10 CM) PANCAKES

3 tablespoons flax meal

½ cup (120 ml) warm water

1 cup (250 g) Classic Peanut Butter (page 29)

2 large ripe bananas, mashed

¾ cup (180 ml) almond milk (see Basic Nut Milk recipe, page 3)

¼ cup (60 ml) pure maple syrup

1 teaspoon vanilla extract

1 cup (112 g) coconut flour

½ cup (50 g) almond pulp or almond meal (see page 58)

2 teaspoons baking powder

½ teaspoon sea salt

2 to 3 tablespoons coconut oil, for greasing pan (see page xix)

1. Whisk together the flax meal and water in a small bowl. Place it in the refrigerator for a minute to set. It will become gummy, like an egg.

2. Mix the peanut butter, bananas, almond milk, maple syrup, and vanilla together in a small saucepan. Stir over medium heat until the ingredients are well combined, 2 to 3 minutes. Remove the mixture from the heat and set it aside to cool a little.

3. While the peanut butter and banana mixture cools, combine the coconut flour, almond pulp, baking powder,

recipe continues

and sea salt together in a large bowl.

4. Once the mixture in the saucepan has cooled to lukewarm, add it to the bowl of dry ingredients and mix well, using either a handheld or stand mixer (both work well).

5. Add the flax/water mixture and stir until the ingredients are well combined. The batter will be much thicker than traditional pancake batter.

6. Add the coconut oil to a large sauté pan over medium heat. Using a ½-cup (120 ml) measure, scoop out the pancake batter. As I previously noted, the batter will be thick, so you'll need to use a spatula to spread it out onto the pan. I find that wetting the spatula with a little water makes it easier to spread the pancakes out. Unlike traditional pancakes, you can't really tell when these are ready to be flipped without looking at the underside. I check them after 1 to 2 minutes, using the spatula to carefully lift up a corner to see if it has turned golden brown yet.

7. Repeat these steps until you've used all of the pancake batter. Since maple syrup is added to the batter, these pancakes are sweet enough to be eaten on their own.

NOTE

If you have any leftover pancakes, store them in an airtight container in the refrigerator or freezer. Place a sheet of parchment paper between each pancake so that they won't stick together. If you store them in the fridge, they should last a week. If you freeze them, they should last several months. To reheat frozen pancakes, let them mostly thaw at room temperature, then gently reheat them in an oven at 350°F (177°C) for 5 minutes, or in a microwave for about 20 seconds.

Variations

There are so many delightful ways you can further enhance this recipe. One idea is to fold ½ cup (60 g) of sliced strawberries or ¼ cup (40 g) of chocolate chips into the batter right before you cook the pancakes. Another fun variation is to drizzle some warm chocolate sauce over them (see Bonus Recipe on the following page).

PREP AND COOK TIME: About 30 minutes

Chocolate Sauce

If you need a good recipe for chocolate sauce, I have your back. Just take ¼ cup (60ml) of melted coconut oil, ¼ cup (30 g) of unsweetened cocoa powder, and 2 to 3 tablespoons of pure maple syrup, and mix it all together. The cocoa powder drowns out most of the coconut flavor, so give it a try even if coconut isn't your thing—it's well worth it. Keep in mind that the coconut oil will solidify after some time at room temperature, so make sure to use the sauce immediately, while it's still warm.

Grain-Free Energy Bites

THESE NO-BAKE energy bites are a great way to utilize leftover hazelnut or almond pulp. They contain enough protein, fat, and sugar to make them an excellent pre- or post-workout snack. My husband even takes them to work for a mid-afternoon pick-me-up. You can also pack them as trail food for a hike, although I recommend freezing them first so that they don't become too soft while you explore.

MAKES FIFTEEN 1½-INCH (4 CM) BITES

1½ cups (150 g) hazelnut pulp or almond pulp (see page 58)

1 cup (90 g) unsweetened shredded coconut

10 to 12 Medjool dates, pits removed

3 to 4 tablespoons water

1. Put all the ingredients into a food processor and mix until a dough forms, 2 to 3 minutes. If it seems a bit dry, add more water. You can also use a high-powered blender, but if so, I highly recommend soaking the dates in water for 30 minutes first in order to soften them enough to be used in a blender.

2. Roll the mixture into bite-size balls and place them on a parchment-lined plate. Refrigerate them for an hour to set.

3. Store the bites in an airtight container in the refrigerator for up to 2 weeks; or in the freezer for up to 6 months.

NOTES

⚜ These energy bites are only mildly sweet, so if you prefer an extra-sweet flavor you'll probably want to add some liquid sweetener. I recommend using 2 tablespoons of pure maple syrup.

⁎ If you don't have leftover pulp from making nut milk, you can use almond meal instead.

PREP AND CHILL TIME: 5 to 10 minutes (not including the soak time for the dates, if using a blender), plus an hour to set in the refrigerator

Protein-Packed Snack Balls

THESE NO-BAKE snack balls are perfect for an extended-energy supply, and provide another great use for almond or hazelnut pulp. Combining chia and flax seeds with the almond butter means that these snacks are full of protein and fiber, and It doesn't hurt that they taste amazing, too. Once you try these, you'll want to make them again and again.

MAKES TWELVE 1½-INCH (4 CM) BALLS

1 cup (150 g) almond pulp or hazelnut pulp (see page 58)

⅓ cup (85 g) almond butter (see Basic Nut Butter recipe, page 26)

3 tablespoons pure maple syrup

2 tablespoons coconut oil (see page xix)

2 tablespoons chia seeds

2 tablespoons flaxseeds

1. Put all the ingredients into a food processor and mix until a dough forms, about 5 minutes.

2. Carefully roll the dough into balls. The dough doesn't hold together very well when rolling it between your hands, but it will firm up again in the refrigerator.

3. Chill in the refrigerator until nice and firm, about 1 hour.

4. Store the balls in an airtight container in the refrigerator for up to 2 weeks, or in the freezer for up to 3 months.

Variation

If you want a little crunch as well as a natural source of caffeine, roll the balls in ¼ cup (30 g) of cacao nibs before you put them in the refrigerator to chill. If you want the same flavor but with a milder kick, fold the cacao nibs into the mixture instead.

PREP AND CHILL TIME: About 10 minutes, plus 1 hour to set in the fridge

Honey Nut Breakfast Cookies

I ABSOLUTELY LOVE making breakfast in cookie form. My two girls, like most other children, can be pretty picky eaters at times. They will, however, eat almost anything if it looks like a cookie. This recipe is one way I'm able to get healthy whole grains into their diet without their knowing. These cookies are packed with a substantial amount of fiber and protein, so they'll keep you full for quite some time. Don't be fooled—this recipe isn't only for kids; adults enjoy the cookies as well. My husband often brings them to work to eat as a mid-morning snack with a cup of coffee.

MAKES FIFTEEN 1½-INCH (4 CM) COOKIES

1 tablespoon flax meal

3 tablespoons warm water

1½ cups (150 g) gluten-free rolled oats

1 cup (100 g) almond pulp or almond meal (see page 58)

⅓ cup (63 g) raw almonds, chopped

½ teaspoon baking powder

½ teaspoon sea salt

⅓ cup (85 g) Classic Peanut Butter (page 29)

½ cup (120 ml) unsweetened applesauce (see page xviii)

⅓ cup (80 ml) raw honey or pure maple syrup

3 tablespoons almond milk (see Basic Nut Milk recipe, page 3)

1 teaspoon vanilla extract

1. Preheat the oven to 350°F (175°C).

2. Whisk together the flax meal and water in a small bowl. Place it in the refrigerator for a minute to set. It will become gummy, like an egg.

3. Combine the oats, almond pulp, chopped almonds, baking powder, and sea salt in a large bowl. Set it aside.

4. Mix the peanut butter, applesauce, honey, almond milk, and vanilla together in a saucepan. Stir over medium-low heat until the ingredients are well combined, 2 to 3 minutes.

recipe continues

5. Add the peanut butter mixture to the dry ingredients and mix well, using either a handheld or stand mixer (both work well), about 2 minutes.

6. Add the flax/water mixture and mix well for another minute.

7. Shape the dough into bite-size balls, slightly flattened, and place them about 1 inch (2.5 cm) apart on a parchment-lined baking sheet.

8. Bake the cookies for 15 to 17 minutes, until the edges look golden. Wait until they've completely cooled before removing them from the baking sheet.

9. Store the cookies in an airtight container in the refrigerator for up to 3 weeks or in the freezer for up to 3 months.

NOTE

If you have a peanut allergy, almond butter can be substituted for the peanut butter. If you're allergic to nuts altogether, you can substitute sunflower seeds for the chopped nuts, Sunflower Seed Milk (page 16) for the almond milk, and Sunflower Seed Butter (page 55) for the peanut butter. Your cookies will come out equally delicious.

PREP AND BAKE TIME:
25 to 30 minutes

Maple Vanilla Almond Granola

GROUND VANILLA BEANS are the true star in this homemade granola, but the almond pulp plays an important supporting role. Sometimes I devour it right off the pan, and it's also good in a bowl with some almond milk (see Basic Nut Milk recipe, page 3) or on top of some yogurt. It usually doesn't last a day in my house, with all the hands sneaking tastes before it's even cooled all the way.

MAKES 4 CUPS (480 G)

3 cups (300 g) gluten-free rolled oats

⅔ cup (65 g) almond pulp or almond meal (see page 58)

½ cup (35 g) chopped almonds

2 teaspoons ground vanilla beans (see page xx)

½ teaspoon sea salt

½ cup (120 ml) unsweetened applesauce (see page xviii)

½ cup (120 ml) pure maple syrup

1. Preheat the oven to 350°F (175°C).

2. Mix the oats, almond pulp, chopped almonds, vanilla, and sea salt in a large bowl. In another smaller bowl, mix the applesauce and maple syrup.

3. Add the wet ingredients to the dry ones slowly and stir until everything is well combined, about 1 to 2 minutes. I use a silicone spatula to mix them by hand.

4. Spread the mixture out evenly onto a parchment-lined baking sheet and bake it for 15 to 20 minutes.

5. Pull the granola out of the oven, shake it around, and place it back in the oven for another 15 to 20 minutes, until golden brown.

recipe continues

6. Store the granola in an airtight container at room temperature for up to a week, in the refrigerator for up to 3 weeks, or in the freezer for up to 3 months.

NOTES

＊ If you like extra-crispy granola, turn the oven temperature down to about 200°F (100°C) and cook it a little longer, checking it every 5 minutes. It will burn easily if you're not careful.

＊ If you don't have access to pure maple syrup, raw honey works fine, although it alters the flavor a bit.

PREP AND BAKE TIME: About 45 minutes

Maple Vanilla Almond Granola

Breakfast

If you asked me what my favorite meal of the day is, I would instantly tell you, breakfast. After fasting all night while I sleep, I appreciate nothing more than a bowl of oats with my morning coffee. But why stop at oatmeal? There are so many ways to incorporate nut milks and butters into your morning routine, and these breakfasts will keep you satisfied and satiated until lunchtime.

Almond Butter and Jelly Muffins

WE MAKE FILLED muffins quite often in our house—they're such a treat for the children (and adults!). My four-year-old daughter refers to them as "muffins with little surprises." Biting into these almond butter muffins to find some jelly waiting inside will make you feel like a kid again. They're perfect to bring to a party or to your office, where they'll quickly disappear after people get a taste.

MAKES 12 MUFFINS

2 tablespoons flax meal

¼ cup plus 2 tablespoons water

2 cups (180 g) gluten-free oat flour (see page xxii)

1 teaspoon baking powder

1 teaspoon baking soda

½ teaspoon sea salt

½ cup (120 g) almond butter (see Basic Nut Butter recipe, page 26)

⅓ cup (80ml) pure maple syrup

¼ cup (60ml) almond milk (see Basic Nut Milk recipe, page 3)

1 teaspoon vanilla extract

½ cup (170 g) your favorite jam (see Bonus Recipe on the following page)

1. Preheat the oven to 350°F (175°C).

2. Whisk together the flax meal and water in a small bowl. Place it in the refrigerator for a minute to set. It will become gummy, like an egg.

3. Mix the oat flour, baking powder, baking soda, and sea salt in a large bowl. Set it aside.

4. Mix the almond butter, maple syrup, almond milk, and vanilla in a saucepan over medium heat. Using a silicone spatula, stir until smooth, about 2 minutes.

5. Add the almond butter mixture and the flax/water mixture to the dry ingredients and mix well, about 1 minute, using either a handheld or stand mixer (both work well).

recipe continues

6. Spoon a little dollop of batter into each cup of a lined or greased muffin pan, filling them about ¼-inch (.6 cm) high. The batter will be very thick because of the almond butter, so I recommend wetting a spoon or spatula to help keep it from sticking. Once a little batter is in the bottom of each cup, use your finger to create a small depression in the middle. This is where the jam will sit. Be careful not to make the hole too deep, or the jam will ooze out the bottom.

7. Spoon a dollop of jam into the indentation.

8. Spoon some more batter into each muffin cup, until they're about three-quarters full.

9. Bake the muffins for 10 to 12 minutes, until a toothpick inserted into the middle comes out clean. Wait for them to cool completely before removing them from the pans.

10. Store the muffins in an airtight container in the refrigerator for up to 2 weeks or in the freezer for up to 6 months.

NOTE

If you're not eating gluten-free, feel free to use whole wheat pastry flour or spelt flour.

PREP AND BAKE TIME:
20 to 25 minutes

BONUS RECIPE

Homemade Jam

I like to make my own jam using 1 cup (150 g) of berries, 1 tablespoon of chia seeds, and 1 teaspoon of pure maple syrup. Mix the ingredients in a food processor for 30 seconds, then place the jam in the fridge for 30 minutes.

Banana Walnut Oatmeal Muffins

IN MY HOUSE breakfast has to be kid-friendly or else I wind up making two meals. These muffins are always greeted with smiling faces by my whole family and never last very long. You can make them ahead of time and freeze them for an easy breakfast on busy days. I pull mine out the night before I want to serve them so that by morning they're perfectly thawed and ready to eat. This recipe yields a small batch, so you might want to double or triple it if you intend to feed more than a few people.

MAKES 3 JUMBO OR 6 STANDARD MUFFINS

3 cups (300 g) gluten-free rolled oats

1 teaspoon cinnamon

½ teaspoon sea salt

2 ripe bananas, mashed

⅓ cup (85 g) walnut butter (see Basic Nut Butter recipe, page 26)

3 tablespoons pure maple syrup

2 to 3 tablespoons almond milk (see Basic Nut Milk recipe, page 3)

1 teaspoon vanilla extract

1. Preheat the oven to 350°F (175°C).

2. Mix the oats, cinnamon, and sea salt together in a large bowl. Set it aside.

3. Mix the banana, walnut butter, maple syrup, almond milk, and vanilla in a small saucepan. Stir over medium heat with a silicone spatula until the ingredients are well combined, about 2 to 3 minutes.

4. Add the banana mixture to the bowl with the oats. Stir until the ingredients are completely mixed, about 1 minute, using either a handheld or stand mixer (both work well).

recipe continues

5. Spoon the mixture into the cups of a lined or greased muffin pan. Bake for 15 to 18 minutes, until slightly golden. Wait until they're completely cooled before removing them from the muffin pan.

6. Store the muffins in the refrigerator for up to 1 week or in the freezer for up to 3 months. I like to keep mine in a ziplock bag.

Variations

* If you want to give these an extra boost, try sprinkling a cinnamon-coconut sugar blend on top of each muffin. Use 1 tablespoon of coconut sugar (see page xix) and ¼ teaspoon of cinnamon.

* This recipe is also delicious when you use almond butter instead of walnut butter, omit the cinnamon, and add ¼ cup (40 g) of chocolate chips.

* Other potential add-ins include 2 tablespoons of shredded coconut, raisins, chia seeds, or hemp seeds.

PREP AND BAKE TIME: About 25 minutes

Banana Walnut Oatmeal Muffins

Banana Muffins with Chocolate Hazelnut Filling

IF YOU'RE A seasoned baker, you probably know that banana breads are a great way to use up bananas that are beginning to brown. These wonderfully moist muffins have been supercharged with a luscious chocolate hazelnut filling. I really don't see how they could get any better than this.

MAKES 12 MUFFINS

1 tablespoon flax meal

3 tablespoons warm water

1¾ cup (160 g) gluten-free oat flour (see page xxii)

1 teaspoon baking powder

½ teaspoon sea salt

2 ripe bananas, mashed

⅓ cup (80 ml) unsweetened applesauce (see page xviii)

¼ cup (60 ml) pure maple syrup

5 tablespoons almond milk (see Basic Nut Milk recipe, page 3)

1 tablespoon coconut oil (see Note on page xix)

1 teaspoon vanilla extract

1 cup (240 g) Chocolate Hazelnut Spread (page 34) or your favorite nut butter for filling (see page 25)

1. Preheat the oven to 350°F (175°C).

2. Whisk together the flax meal and water in a small bowl. Place it in the refrigerator for a minute to set. It will become gummy, like an egg.

3. Mix the oat flour, baking powder, and sea salt in a large bowl.

4. Mix the bananas, applesauce, maple syrup, almond milk, coconut oil, and vanilla in a small saucepan. Stir over medium heat with a silicone spatula until all the ingredients are well combined, 2 to 3 minutes.

5. Add the banana mixture to the bowl with the oats. Stir until the ingredients are completely mixed, 1 to 2 minutes.

recipe continues

6. Add the flax/water mixture and mix well, using either a handheld or stand mixer (both work well).

7. Spoon a small amount of batter into the bottom of each cup in a lined or greased muffin pan. Add a dollop of the Chocolate Hazelnut Spread on top, then fill each cup with more muffin batter until they're about three-quarters full.

8. Bake the muffins for 12 to 15 minutes, until golden. Wait until the muffins have completely cooled before removing them from the pans.

9. Store the muffins in an airtight container at room temperature for up to 4 days, for up to 2 weeks in the refrigerator, or for up to 6 months in the freezer.

Variation

Try making these with almond butter or cashew butter, which are equally delicious.

PREP AND BAKE TIME:
20 to 25 minutes

Peanut Butter Cup Granola

BEFORE I STARTED down my whole-food journey, I adored peanut butter cups. I remember going to chocolatiers when I lived in Las Vegas, looking for the perfect peanut butter cup to devour. Although I'm no longer on a search for the perfect peanut butter cup, I made this recipe to incorporate my love of everything peanut butter cup into my morning meal. It might be a breakfast food, but I promise it tastes like you're eating dessert. And who doesn't like a little something sweet to start the day? This dish will give you something to look forward to when you go to bed at night.

MAKES 4 CUPS (480 G)

3 cups (300 g) gluten-free rolled oats

3 tablespoons unsweetened cocoa powder or cacao powder

1 teaspoon sea salt

½ cup (125 g) Classic Peanut Butter (page 29)

⅓ cup (80ml) pure maple syrup

¼ cup (60ml) unsweetened applesauce (see page xviii)

2 tablespoons almond milk (see Basic Nut Milk recipe, page 3)

1 teaspoon ground vanilla beans or vanilla extract (see page xx)

1. Preheat the oven to 350°F (175°C).

2. Mix together the oats, cocoa powder, and sea salt in a large bowl.

3. Mix the peanut butter, maple syrup, applesauce, almond milk, and vanilla in a small saucepan. Stir over medium heat using a silicone spatula until the ingredients are well combined, about 2 minutes.

4. Add the peanut butter mixture to the bowl with the oats and stir with the spatula until everything is well coated.

recipe continues

5. Spread the mixture out evenly onto a parchment-lined baking sheet and bake for about 25 minutes, stopping halfway through to shake the granola around a bit. You can tell it's ready when the granola has a golden color to it.

6. Wait until the granola is completely cooled before removing it from the baking sheet.

7. Store the granola in an airtight container at room temperature for up to 7 days, in the refrigerator for up to 2 weeks, or in the freezer for up to 6 months.

PREP AND BAKE TIME: About 35 minutes

BONUS RECIPE

Peanut Butter Cup Granola Cookies

You can easily turn this recipe into cookies. All you need to do is add another ¼ cup (60 g) of peanut butter. After mixing, drop scoops of the batter onto a parchment-lined baking sheet and bake for 15 minutes. It's hard to visually tell when these are done, so I lightly press my finger into a cookie to feel if it's firm enough. Use a cookie scoop or two spoons to drop the cookies onto the baking sheet; either method works fine.

Peanut Butter Cup Granola

Peanut Butter Chocolate Chip Donuts

DID SOMEONE SAY donuts? Yes, please! These iconic American breakfast (well, possibly dessert) treats bring a smile to everyone's face. My husband loves donuts so much that he takes off for the closest donut shop whenever I turn my back. Okay, maybe that's an exaggeration, but I promise, it would be impossible for him to live without the occasional donut. So I created these peanut butter chocolate chip versions for him to have at home. Donuts are traditionally deep fried in peanut or vegetable oil, but to make mine a bit healthier than their store-bought counterparts, I bake them to avoid the grease overload. I'll bet you'll get hooked on these the first time you try them, just like my family did.

MAKES 12 DONUTS

½ cup (120 ml) unsweetened applesauce (see page xviii)

⅓ cup (80 ml) pure maple syrup

½ cup (125 g) Classic Peanut Butter (page 29)

3 tablespoons almond milk (see Basic Nut Milk recipe, page 3)

1 teaspoon vanilla extract

2 cups (180 g) gluten-free oat flour (see page xxii)

1 teaspoon baking powder

½ teaspoon sea salt

⅓ cup (50 g) dark chocolate chips

1. Preheat the oven to 350°F (175°C).

2. Mix the applesauce, maple syrup, peanut butter, almond milk, and vanilla in a small saucepan. Stir over medium heat until the ingredients are well combined, 2 to 3 minutes. Remove the mixture from the heat and let it cool for 5 minutes.

3. While the applesauce mixture cools, mix together the oat flour, baking powder, and sea salt in a large bowl.

recipe continues

4. When the applesauce mixture has cooled, add it to the dry ingredients and mix well, using either a handheld or stand mixer (both work well).

5. Fold in the chocolate chips with a spoon or spatula.

6. Spoon the batter into greased donut pans and bake for 10 minutes, until golden. Let the donuts cool completely before removing them from the pans.

7. Store the donuts in the refrigerator for at least a week, if not a few days more, or in the freezer for up to 3 months. To defrost, pull them out the night before and let them thaw at room temperature overnight.

NOTE

If you don't have donut pans, you can make this recipe in a standard muffin pan. Simply cook them a few extra minutes to allow the centers to cook through. They turn out just as tasty.

PREP AND BAKE TIME:

20 to 25 minutes

Four-Ingredient Almond Butter Breakfast Cookies

IF BAKING ISN'T your thing, whether it intimidates you or you're new to it, this is one of the easiest recipes you could ever make. If you're a seasoned professional, these cookies will remind you that simple food can be exquisite. One of the best things about this recipe is that you probably already have all the ingredients you need on hand! So step into the kitchen and get busy—you'll be finished in no time.

MAKES SIXTEEN 2-INCH (5 CM) COOKIES

2 cups (200 g) gluten-free rolled oats

½ teaspoon sea salt

2 bananas, mashed

1 cup (240 g) almond butter (see Basic Nut Butter recipe, page 26)

2 tablespoons pure maple syrup, optional

1. Preheat the oven to 350°F (175°C).

2. Mix the oats and sea salt in a large bowl.

3. Mix the bananas with the almond butter and maple syrup (if you choose to use it) in a small saucepan. Cook over medium heat, stirring constantly, until the ingredients are mixed well, about 2 minutes.

4. Add the banana mixture to the oats and mix until the ingredients are well combined, using either a handheld or stand mixer (both work well), or mix it by hand with a silicone spatula.

recipe continues

5. Using a cookie scoop or two spoons, drop dollops of the dough onto a parchment-lined baking sheet, about 1 inch apart.

6. Bake the cookies for 10 minutes, until lightly golden. Let them completely cool before removing them from the baking sheet.

7. Store the cookies in an airtight container in the refrigerator for up to 2 weeks, or in the freezer for up to 6 months.

NOTE

For an added boost of protein, add 2 tablespoons of chia seeds or hemp hearts (shelled hemp seeds).

PREP AND BAKE TIME: About 15 minutes

**Four-Ingredient Almond
Butter Breakfast Cookies**

Pecan "Caramel" Overnight Oats

IMAGINE A BREAKFAST that takes only minutes to make, requires no cooking, and will leave you satisfied for hours. It exists! Overnight oats are my favorite breakfast, partly because of the endless number of flavor combinations you can enjoy. I make five jars' worth at a time for easy breakfast options all week. It makes having a healthy meal and still getting out the door on time on weekday mornings easy.

MAKES ONE 12-OUNCE (340 G) SERVING

½ cup (150 g) gluten-free rolled oats or gluten-free steel-cut oats

2 teaspoons chia seeds

1 teaspoon cinnamon

½ to ¾ cup (125 to 180 ml) almond milk (amount depends on how thick you like your oatmeal; see Basic Nut Milk recipe, page 3)

1 tablespoon pecan butter (see Basic Nut Butter recipe, page 26)

1 Medjool date, pit removed and finely chopped

1. Mix the oats, chia seeds, and cinnamon together in a glass jar that holds at least 12 ounces (340 ml). I prefer mason jars, but you can use any kind you like; recycled jam jars work well, too.

2. Add the almond milk, peanut butter, and chopped date, and stir until the ingredients are well combined. Make sure to blend the pecan butter evenly inside the jar. I use the back of my spoon to break up any chunks while I'm stirring.

3. Store the oats covered overnight in the refrigerator. Make sure to mix them well in the morning just before eating.

NOTES

* Steel-cuts oats will still retain a crunch in the morning, which I enjoy. You can use rolled oats if you prefer a smoother oatmeal. Don't use quick oats; they get too soggy.

* If you're sensitive to oats, you can use millet instead.

* Instead of the date, you can use 2 teaspoons of pure maple syrup, although it won't have as much of a caramel-like texture and taste.

* This oatmeal also works well warmed up. Heat it in the microwave for no more than 30 seconds, or place the jar in a pot of water and heat it gently on the stove.

Variations

* A great alteration to this recipe is to substitute almond butter (see Basic Nut Butter recipe, page 26) for the pecan butter, omit the cinnamon, and add 2 teaspoons of unsweetened cocoa powder or cacao powder.

* I also like to add 1 to 2 teaspoons of maca powder to this recipe for a natural energy boost!

PREP TIME: About 5 minutes (not including the overnight soak)

Pecan "Caramel" Overnight Oats,
page 94

Triple Berry Chia Seed Pudding,
page 98

Triple Berry Chia Seed Pudding

IN THE 1980S chia seeds were something you spread over a ceramic animal to watch them sprout. Today they're recognized as an ancient Aztec superfood. Did you know that one serving of chia seeds contains 11 grams of fiber? That's 42 percent of the daily recommendation! They're also a great source of protein and healthy fats. With their high fiber content, they'll keep you satiated for a long time. Since they expand in liquid, a little goes a long way, and they fill you up more than you might think. There are so many ways to eat chia seeds, but my favorite is in pudding, like in this simple recipe. You can even easily take it on the go!

MAKES FOUR ½-CUP (250 G) SERVINGS

2 cups (480 ml) Brazil nut milk (see Basic Nut Milk recipe, page 3)

½ cup (80 g) chia seeds

½ cup (47 g) shredded unsweetened coconut

1 cup (125 g) sliced strawberries (see Notes on the following page)

1 cup (150 g) blueberries (see Notes on the following page)

½ cup (70 g) blackberries (see Notes on the following page)

1 teaspoon ground vanilla beans (see page xx)

3 tablespoons pure maple syrup

1. Place all the ingredients in a large bowl and mix them very well. The chia seeds have a tendency to clump together at the bottom of the bowl, so make sure to stir completely for several minutes. Using a silicone spatula helps blend those stubborn chia seeds at the bottom.

2. Place the bowl, covered, in the refrigerator for 4 hours to firm up. The pudding should last in the refrigerator for 4 to 5 days.

NOTES

* Chia seeds have a texture similar to tapioca, although the seeds are much smaller. If you're not a fan of the texture, after the seeds have expanded, throw the whole mixture into a blender and mix it to a smoother texture.

* You can use fresh or frozen berries for this recipe. If you use frozen ones, make sure they're completely thawed before mixing.

PREP AND CHILL TIME: About 5 minutes, plus 4 hours to set in the fridge

Smoothies

The perfect breakfast for those on the go, or a delicious treat any time of the day, smoothies can go in countless directions: vibrant and green, healthfully protein-packed, rich and dessert-like, refreshingly fruity. The possibilities are endless. I'm pleased to share several different smoothie recipes that are sure to put a smile on your face. If you want to add a protein boost to your smoothies, I suggest adding a few tablespoons of oats, chia seeds, hemp seeds, or nuts. You can use a protein powder if you wish, but I try to get my protein from natural sources, since most protein powders are highly processed, compromising the nutrients.

Strawberry Banana Green Smoothie

ONE OF THE most classic green smoothie recipes, this delectable combination of strawberries and bananas makes it hard to resist. If you're new to green smoothies, this is a great one to start with, since the fruit masks any flavor from the greens. My kids eat this up and have no idea they're getting a hidden serving of veggies. You don't have to use the goji berries, although I really enjoy the flavor they bring to this smoothie, not to mention that they contain high amounts of vitamin A and antioxidants and are very good for you. If you're not a fan of spinach, don't worry — you can't taste it at all.

MAKES 10 OUNCES (295ML)

1 cup (240 ml) Brazil nut milk (see Basic Nut Milk recipe, page 3)

2 cups (20 g) loosely packed spinach

1 frozen banana (see page 104)

1 cup (220 g) frozen strawberries

1 tablespoon dried goji berries

1. Mix the Brazil nut milk and the spinach well in a high powered blender on medium speed, about 2 minutes. You might need to stop and scrape down the sides of the canister a few times. It's important to do this step first to make sure the spinach breaks down completely so that you don't end up with chunks of greenery in your drink.

2. Add the fruit and continue to blend well, 1 to 2 minutes.

3. Serve immediately, or refrigerate for up to 24 hours. You can also pour the smoothie into ice

recipe continues

cube trays and freeze it for up to 6 months. To use, just throw some of the frozen cubes back into the blender for a minute.

NOTES

* If you'd like to increase the protein in this smoothie, add 2 tablespoons of hemp seeds, chia seeds, oats, or nuts. If you prefer protein powder, feel free to use that as well; just add the serving amount listed on your container.

* I highly recommend using a high-powered blender for green smoothies, since it does the best job of breaking up the greens.
* When I freeze bananas, I simply peel them and put them in a ziplock bag. Then I slice the banana into small pieces right before putting it into the blender.

PREP TIME: About 5 minutes

Chocolate Almond Butter Smoothie

THIS DECADENT YET nutritious smoothie makes a healthy breakfast and is indulgent enough for dessert as well. I like to pour the mixture into ice-pop molds and stick them in the freezer to enjoy with my kids on hot summer days.

MAKES 2 CUPS (480 ML)

½ to 1 cup (20 g) almond milk (see Basic Nut Milk recipe, page 3)

1 cup (240 ml) loosely packed fresh spinach

2 frozen bananas (see page 104)

2 tablespoons almond butter (see Basic Nut Butter recipe, page 26)

1 heaping tablespoon unsweetened cocoa powder

1 tablespoon chia seeds

1. Mix the almond milk and spinach well in a high-powered blender on medium speed, about 2 minutes. Make sure to break up the greens thoroughly to avoid big chunks in your drink.

2. Add the remaining ingredients and blend for another 1 to 2 minutes, until the smoothie reaches the consistency you desire.

3. Serve immediately, or refrigerate for up to 24 hours. You can also pour the smoothie mixture into ice cube trays and freeze it for up to 6 months. To use, just put some of the frozen cubes back into the blender for a minute.

NOTE

In place of the almond butter you can substitute another nut butter or Sunflower Seed Butter (page 55) if you prefer.

PREP TIME: About 5 minutes

**Chocolate Almond Butter Smoothie,
page 105**

Mixed Berry and Kale Smoothie,
page 108

Mixed Berry and Kale Smoothie

KALE SEEMS TO be the superfood everyone's talking about these days. However, the taste can take a bit of getting used to. Smoothies are a great way to get some of this nutritious green into your diet without really tasting it at all. Any of the many varieties of kale work in this recipe; I like red kale the best, but feel free to substitute your own personal favorite. If you're sensitive to the taste, I suggest using baby kale, which is much milder.

MAKES 1 CUP (240 ML)

1 cup (240 ml) almond milk (see Basic Nut Milk recipe, page 3)

2 cups (20 g) loosely packed fresh kale, stalks removed

2 cups (460 g) frozen mixed berries

1. Mix the almond milk and the kale in a high-powered blender, starting on a low speed and working up to high, until well blended, about 2 minutes. You can do this in a regular blender, but a high-powered blender does a better job of breaking up the greens.

2. Add the berries and blend for another minute or so, until the smoothie reaches the consistency you desire.

3. Serve immediately, or refrigerate for up to 24 hours. You can also pour the smoothie into ice cube trays and freeze it for up to 6 months. To use, just put some of the frozen cubes back into the blender for a minute.

NOTES

* If you don't care for kale, 2 cups (20 g) of spinach or Swiss chard, loosely packed, with stalks removed, makes a great replacement.
* If you juice at home, save the stalks for juicing later, since they hold most of the liquid from the leaf.

PREP TIME: About 5 minutes

Superfood Chocolate Smoothie

AVOCADOS MAKE EVERYTHING a little better. This delicious and superhealthy smoothie is no exception. Avocado lends an extra-special creaminess, and the chia seeds expand to help keep you full. With cacao powder you get the added health benefits of using chocolate in one of its purest forms.

MAKES 4 CUPS (960 ML)

2½ cups (600 ml) almond milk (see Basic Nut Milk recipe, page 3)

2 frozen bananas (see page 104)

1 ripe avocado (skin and seed removed)

2 tablespoons cacao powder or unsweetened cocoa powder

1 tablespoon chia seeds

2 Medjool dates, pits removed

1. Add the almond milk, banana, and avocado to a high-powered blender. Blend on high speed for about 2 minutes, until creamy and well mixed.

2. Add the cacao powder, chia seeds, and dates and blend for 1 to 2 minutes, until the smoothie reaches the consistency you desire.

3. Serve immediately, or refrigerate for up to 24 hours. You can also pour the smoothie into ice cube trays and freeze it for up to 6 months. To use, just throw some of the frozen cubes back into the blender for a minute.

NOTE

To give this smoothie an extra boost, add 2 tablespoons of dried goji berries.

PREP TIME: About 5 minutes

**Superfood Chocolate Smoothie,
page 109**

**Tropical Protein Smoothie,
page 112**

Tropical Protein Smoothie

THIS SMOOTHIE IS quite the breakfast treat. Who needs protein powder when almond pulp can give you a natural protein boost? And why reach for refined sugar to sweeten your breakfast when the refreshing flavors of pineapple, banana, and mango will satisfy any sweet tooth? With all of these benefits, plus the high fiber from the almond pulp, you should be kept full and content until lunchtime with this tropical smoothie.

MAKES 2 CUPS (480 ML)

1 cup (240 ml) almond milk (see Basic Nut Milk recipe, page 3)

¼ cup (25 g) almond pulp (see How to Use Nut Pulp, page 57, and Note on the following page)

1 frozen banana (see page 104)

1 cup (245 g) frozen pineapple

½ cup (75 g) frozen mango

1. Combine the almond milk and pulp in a high-powered blender and blend for 2 minutes. If you have a variable-speed blender, I suggest starting at a low speed and working your way up to high. Make sure to blend the ingredients well.

2. Add the remaining ingredients and continue to blend until the mixture is smooth, about another 2 minutes.

3. Serve immediately, or refrigerate for up to 24 hours. You can also pour the smoothie into ice cube trays and freeze it for up to 6 months. To make a quick breakfast on busy mornings, just throw some of the frozen cubes back into the blender for a minute.

NOTE

If you don't have any almond pulp,
substitute almond meal or even
2 tablespoons of ground raw almonds.

Variation

If you want to mix some greens in
with this, I suggest adding 1 cup
(20 g) of greens (spinach, kale, or
any other kind), loosely packed, at
the same time you add the milk and
almond pulp.

PREP TIME: About 5 minutes

Peanut Butter and Jelly Smoothie

PEANUT BUTTER AND jelly is a staple in most children's diets, so why not turn it into a smoothie? This recipe makes the perfect kid-friendly breakfast for on-the-go mornings. Filled with fiber, protein, and a little sweetness, this will keep your kids full until lunchtime, then have them coming back for more. In our house, even my husband comes back for more!—maybe because he's a kid at heart!

MAKES 1 CUP (240 ML)

1 cup (240 ml) almond milk (see Basic Nut Milk recipe, page 3)

1 frozen banana (see page 104)

1 cup (150 g) frozen blueberries or strawberries

2 tablespoons Classic Peanut Butter (page 29)

1. Combine all the ingredients in a high-powered blender. Blend on high speed until smooth, 1 to 2 minutes.

2. Serve immediately, or refrigerate for up to 24 hours. You can also pour the smoothie into ice cube trays and freeze it for up to 6 months. To use, just throw some of the frozen cubes back into the blender for a minute.

NOTE

If you want to add an extra kick of protein and fiber to this drink, add 1 tablespoon of chia seeds.

PREP TIME: About 3 minutes

Oranges and Cream Smoothie

AS A LITTLE girl, one of my favorite desserts was a Creamsicle. That tangy orange outside with a creamy vanilla center—what kid doesn't love them? I tried to recreate those flavors here in a healthier way. I chose Brazil nut milk to use in this smoothie because of its incredibly creamy texture.

MAKES 4 CUPS (960 ML)

1 cup (240 ml) Brazil nut milk (see Basic Nut Milk recipe, page 3)

1 cup (140 g) ice

2 large carrots, peeled and chopped into small circles

2 Medjool dates, pits removed

1½ large oranges, such as navel, or 3 small oranges, such as mandarin, peeled and cut into segments

1. Add all the ingredients to a blender and blend for 2 to 3 minutes, until the smoothie reaches the consistency you desire.

2. Serve immediately, or refrigerate for up to 24 hours. You can also pour the smoothie into ice cube trays and freeze it for up to 6 months. To use, just put some of the frozen cubes back into the blender for a minute.

Variation

If you want to make this even more fun for kids to eat, you can pour the smoothie mixture into ice pop molds and freeze them. They should take about 6 hours to set, and then your kids can enjoy yummy ice pops with a hidden serving of veggies inside.

PREP TIME: About 5 minutes

Apple Pie Smoothie

IF YOU WANT to enjoy apple pie for breakfast without the guilt, try this smoothie. It has the taste of apple pie but with far fewer calories! Many apple varieties will work in this recipe, I like Honeycrisps because they're so sweet and full of flavor. Cortland or Gala apples also work beautifully. If you like a little more tartness, try McIntosh or Granny Smith.

MAKES 3½ CUPS (840 ML)

1½ cups (360 ml) cashew milk (see Basic Nut Milk recipe, page 3)

1½ cups (210 g) ice

2 large apples, cored and cut into quarters

1 to 2 Medjool dates, pits removed

1½ teaspoons cinnamon

¼ teaspoon ground nutmeg, optional

1. Mix all the ingredients in a high-powered blender on high speed for 1 to 2 minutes, until the smoothie reaches the consistency you desire.

2. Serve immediately, or refrigerate for up to 24 hours. You can also pour the smoothie into ice cube trays and freeze it for up to 6 months. To use, just put some of the frozen cubes back into the blender for a minute.

PREP TIME: About 5 minutes

No-Bake Treats

Did you know that most fruits, vegetables, seeds, and nuts are more nutritious in their raw state? Cooking or processing whole foods often depletes some of the precious nutrients we need for good health. When it comes to raw desserts, nuts and seeds are the stars, and they usually form the main base for cookies, fudge, tarts, and truffles. In this chapter you'll see how much variety these few simple ingredients can provide. Once you become used to not baking your desserts, it'll be a "piece of cake" to whip up sweet treats that everyone will love. If there's one recipe in this section you shouldn't miss, it's for the Chocolate Almond Banana Cups (page 145), which were featured on the *Today* show.

Strawberry Tarts with Cashew Cream

SPRING IS MY favorite time of year, especially since all the best seasonal fruits start to become available then. One of the absolute best things about springtime has to be the strawberries. Since I try to buy produce only in season, when strawberries begin to pop up, I take full advantage. I included this recipe to demonstrate two things: tarts are pretty easy to make, and cashew cream is delicious and versatile. I hope you enjoy these as much as my family does.

MAKES FOUR 4-INCH (10 CM) MINI-TARTS

FOR THE CRUST:

1 cup (125 g) raw, unsalted almonds

1 cup (100 g) raw, unsalted walnuts

½ teaspoon sea salt

8 Medjool dates, pits removed

2 tablespoons water

Oil, to grease the tart pan (I use coconut oil, but any kind will do)

FOR THE FILLING:

2 cups (260 g) raw, unsalted cashews, soaked overnight (see page xxix)

¼ cup (60 ml) almond milk (see Basic Nut Milk recipe, page 3)

2 to 3 tablespoons pure maple syrup

2 teaspoons ground vanilla beans (see page xx)

1½ cups (180 g) sliced strawberries (see Notes on the following page)

1. To make the crust, put the almonds, walnuts, and sea salt in a food processor. Pulse until the mixture has a coarse consistency, about 1 to 2 minutes. Add the dates and water and pulse until a dough starts to form. This will take another minute or so.

2. Grease the tart pans with a little oil. I use pans with detachable bottoms, which makes the tarts much easier to remove when you're ready to serve them.

3. Gently press the dough mixture into the greased tart shells, to about ¼-inch (.6 cm) thickness. Once all

recipe continues

of the dough has been evenly distributed and pressed into the pans, stick them into the fridge to firm up.

4. While the tart shells set, make the filling: Drain and rinse the cashews. Place them in a high-powered blender with the almond milk, maple syrup, and vanilla. Blend on high speed until smooth, 2 to 3 minutes.

5. Spoon the cashew cream mixture into each tart shell, then top with sliced strawberries. Serve immediately, or store in the refrigerator for up to a week (see Notes below).

NOTES

* You can use either fresh or frozen strawberries in this recipe. If you're using frozen berries, you'll need to let them thaw first. I set mine out on the counter and let them gently defrost for about an hour.

* These tarts are best when the cashew cream is fresh. Once the cream sits in the fridge for a while, it starts to harden a bit. It's still very good like this, but the "cream" will be thicker and start to resemble a nut butter consistency. If you plan on featuring the tarts at a party, make the shells ahead of time, and then blend the cashew cream right before serving them.

* If you can't find ground vanilla beans, use 1 teaspoon of vanilla extract instead. You can also use a whole vanilla bean; just slit the pod open and scrape the seeds into the mixture, then incorporate them fully. Don't throw away the pod, since it can be used to add flavor to sauces and milks.

PREP AND CHILL TIME: 20 minutes (not including the overnight soak for the cashews)

Chocolate Hazelnut Coconut Tart

TARTS, A STAPLE dessert in the raw food world, can be filled with fruit, chocolate, nut spread, or whatever else comes to mind. They might look fancy, but they're actually easy to put together. Making them is mainly about having the proper tools. I strongly suggest using a tart pan with a removable bottom so that when you're ready to serve, you can just lift out the tart with a little care, and voilà! You have a beautiful tart that took minutes to make, with an even quicker presentation.

MAKES ONE 9-INCH (23 CM) TART

FOR THE CRUST:

1 cup (140 g) raw, unsalted Brazil nuts

1 cup (100 g) raw, unsalted walnuts

½ cup (65 g) flax meal

½ teaspoon sea salt

8 to 10 Medjool dates, pits removed

2 to 3 tablespoons water

FOR THE FILLING:

1 cup (240 g) Chocolate Hazelnut Spread (page 34)

1 cup (200 g) coconut butter (see page xxii)

¼ cup (60 ml) almond milk (see Basic Nut Milk recipe, page 3)

FOR THE WHIPPED CREAM TOPPING:

One 14-ounce (400 ml) can full-fat coconut milk, refrigerated overnight

(see Coconut Whipped Cream, page 21)

1 tablespoon pure maple syrup

1 teaspoon ground vanilla bean or vanilla extract (see page xx)

1. To make the crust, combine the Brazil nuts, walnuts, flax meal, and sea salt in a food processor. Pulse until the mixture has a coarse consistency, about 2 minutes. Add the dates and pulse another 2 minutes, then add the water and pulse until a dough forms, another minute or so.

recipe continues

2. Carefully press the dough into a greased 9-inch (23 cm) tart shell. Once it has been pressed evenly into the tart shell, place it in the fridge. It doesn't take long for the crust to set, about 10 minutes. By the time you're finished making the filling, the crust should be ready.

3. While the crust is setting in the fridge, make the filling: Combine all the filling ingredients in a blender and mix until smooth, about 3 to 5 minutes.

4. Once the filling is completely mixed, spread it evenly into the tart crust, using a silicone spatula. The mixture will be slightly thick but spreadable. If it seems a little too sticky, wet the spatula a bit. Place the tart back in the fridge while you make the whipped cream topping.

5. To create the whipped cream topping, make the Coconut Whipped Cream according to the directions on page 21, adding the maple syrup and vanilla to the bowl with the coconut milk fat before whipping everything together.

6. To pipe the whipped cream into the tart, simply transfer it to a ziplock bag, then cut a small hole in one of the corners. Slowly squeeze the cream out a little at a time to decorate the tart any way you wish.

7. Serve immediately, or store in the refrigerator for up to a week (see Note below).

NOTE

If you're topping this tart with the coconut whipped cream, I highly suggest adding it right before serving. Once the coconut whipped cream is stored in the fridge, it will begin to harden.

Variation

This tart also looks beautiful topped with raspberries or strawberries.

PREP AND CHILL TIME: About 20 minutes (not including the overnight refrigeration of the coconut milk)

Chocolate Hazelnut Coconut Tart

Salted Honey Cashew Truffles

WHEN I THINK of truffles, I imagine high-end chocolate shops. Truffles seem so decadent, like something only a well-trained professional could make. The truth is, though, it's super easy to create amazing truffles with a crunchy, chocolaty shell and a sweet surprise inside. This recipe features a buttery, velvety-smooth filling that will literally melt right in your mouth. It's pure bliss, I promise.

MAKES EIGHT 1-INCH (2.5 CM) TRUFFLES

1 cup (240 g) cashew butter (see Basic Nut Butter recipe, page 26)

2 tablespoons raw honey or pure maple syrup

1 teaspoon ground vanilla beans (see page xx)

½ teaspoon sea salt

One 3-ounce (85 g) dark chocolate bar or 1 cup (160 g) dark chocolate chips

3 tablespoons almond milk (see Basic Nut Milk recipe, page 3)

1. Combine the cashew butter, honey, vanilla, and sea salt in a food processor. Pulse until the ingredients are well mixed, 2 to 3 minutes.

2. Roll the mixture into bite-size balls by hand, or use a cookie scoop to make them. I've tried both methods and come out with eight truffles each way. I do find that the cookie scoop keeps things neater, though.

3. Place the balls on a parchment-lined baking sheet, and stick them into the freezer for at least an hour to harden.

4. While the cashew balls are freezing, heat the chocolate and the

recipe continues

milk in a double boiler (see Notes in the next column) over medium-high heat. Stir constantly until all the chocolate is melted, about 5 minutes.

5. Using two forks, roll the frozen cashew balls in the chocolate, working quickly so that the cashew butter doesn't melt, then place them back on the parchment-lined baking sheet. Once all the balls are coated in chocolate, transfer them to the freezer for 3 hours so that the chocolate coating can firm up.

6. Store the truffles in an airtight container in the fridge for up to 2 weeks.

NOTES

* The cashew butter might seem as if it doesn't want to stick together as you roll it, but it will firm up while chilling in the freezer.

* To create a double boiler, fill a medium saucepan with water and bring it to a boil. Once the water is boiling, place a heatproof glass bowl on top of the boiling pot of water. Add the chocolate and almond milk to the glass bowl to gently melt the chocolate without burning it.

PREP AND CHILL TIME: About 30 minutes, plus 4 hours for chilling the truffles

White Chocolate Coconut Fudge

ALTHOUGH I DON'T talk about being a vegan all that often, I do follow that lifestyle. One thing I thought I would have to give up when I went vegan was white chocolate. For almost two years I didn't touch the stuff. One day I simply couldn't take it anymore. I had to have some. So I developed my own alternative. I'm here to tell you that, yes, you can enjoy the taste of white chocolate on a vegan, whole-food diet without feeling guilty—just try this recipe.

MAKES SIX 2½-INCH (6.4 CM) OR TWELVE 1¼-INCH (4 CM) PIECES

1 cup (130 g) raw cashews or ½ cup (120 ml) cashew butter (see Basic Nut Butter recipe, page 26, and Note on the following page)

1 cup (200 g) coconut butter (see page xxii)

½ cup (220 g) cocoa butter

¼ cup (60ml) pure maple syrup

¼ teaspoon sea salt

2 teaspoons ground vanilla bean or 1 teaspoon vanilla extract (see page xx)

1. Chop the cashews in a blender or food processor until they are very fine. It should take 2 to 3 minutes.

2. Mix the coconut butter, cocoa butter, maple syrup, cashews, sea salt, and vanilla in a small saucepan. Stir over medium heat until the ingredients are well combined and the cocoa butter has melted, 3 to 5 minutes.

3. Spoon the mixture into the cups of a lined or greased muffin pan until each cup is about three-quarters full. I like to use a standard muffin pan with silicone liners, although paper liners work, too. If you use

recipe continues

standard muffin pans, you'll get 6 large pieces of fudge; mini-muffin pans will give you 12 small pieces. Another option is to use chocolate molds. If you go this route, be sure to grease the molds first to ensure the fudge comes out easily.

4. Stick the fudge into the freezer for about 40 minutes or into the fridge for about 3 hours to firm up. Once firm, store the pieces of fudge in the fridge for up to 2 weeks, or in the freezer for up to 3 months. If you freeze the fudge, you'll need to let it thaw for about 5 minutes before eating.

NOTE

* If you'd like to use cashew butter instead of raw cashews, cut the amount by half, to ½ cup (120 g) of cashew butter.

* If you don't have muffin pans or chocolate molds, line an 8 x 8-inch (20 cm x 20 cm) baking pan with parchment paper and spread the fudge mixture into it evenly. Cut it into bars or squares once the fudge has set.

Variation

To make coconut almond fudge, omit the cocoa butter, substitute almond butter for the cashews, add 2 tablespoons of coconut oil (see page xix), and ½ teaspoon of almond extract.

PREP AND CHILL TIME: About 40 minutes if chilling fudge in the freezer; up to 3 hours if chilling fudge in the refrigerator.

White Chocolate Coconut Fudge

Chocolate Peanut Butter Fudge

IT'S AMAZING HOW much these little gems taste like traditional dairy fudge. Coconut butter is the perfect choice to give this vegan fudge a velvety texture. If you're not a fan of coconut, don't worry—the flavors of the chocolate and peanut butter almost completely mask the coconut. In fact, the first time my family tried this recipe, they didn't even know it included coconut. The only role it plays in this fudge is giving it an appropriate texture. We all know peanut butter and chocolate were made for each other, so go ahead and dive in!

MAKES TWELVE 2½-INCH (6.4 CM) PIECES

One 3.5 ounce (100 g) dark chocolate bar, roughly chopped, or 1 cup (160 g) dark chocolate chips

1 cup (250 g) Classic Peanut Butter (page 29)

½ cup (100 g) coconut butter (see page xxii)

¾ cup (180 ml) almond milk (see Basic Nut Milk recipe, page 3)

¼ cup pure maple syrup

1. Mix all the ingredients in a medium saucepan. Stir over medium heat until they are well combined, about 2 minutes.

2. Spoon the mixture into 12 lined or greased muffin cups. I use standard size-muffin pans with silicone liners, although paper liners will also work. If you want to make 24 smaller pieces, use a mini muffin pan instead. If you don't have muffin pans, make this fudge in an 8 x 8-inch (20 cm x 20 cm) glass baking dish lined with parchment paper.

3. Stick the fudge into the fridge to set. It should take about 30 minutes to 1 hour.

4. Store the fudge in the refrigerator for up to 3 weeks, or in the freezer for up to 3 months. If you keep it in the freezer, you'll need to let it thaw slightly, about 5 minutes, before eating.

PREP AND CHILL TIME: 30 minutes to 1 hour

Almond Butter Mousse

MY HUSBAND AND I were on vacation in Austin, Texas, one summer, sampling the local fare and talking about recipes to make for the blog. We had the good fortune of eating a vegan mousse on that trip, and from that delightful treat this recipe was born. It's a fancy dessert that takes very little effort to make, so you can wow your guests with a rich mousse in minutes.

MAKES FOUR ½-CUP (120 G) SERVINGS

One 14-ounce (400 ml) can full-fat coconut milk, refrigerated overnight

½ cup (120 g) almond butter (see Basic Nut Butter recipe, page 26)

¼ cup (60ml) almond milk (see Basic Nut Milk recipe, page 3)

2 tablespoons pure maple syrup

1 teaspoon vanilla extract

1. Stick an unopened can of coconut milk into the fridge the night before you plan to make this recipe. When you open it the next morning, the fatty part of the coconut milk will have separated from the water.

2. Spoon out the fatty part of the coconut milk into a large mixing bowl. Freeze the leftover coconut water in ice cube trays to add to smoothies in the future (see page 101).

3. Mix the almond butter, almond milk, maple syrup, and vanilla in a small saucepan. Stir over medium heat until the ingredients are just combined, about 2 minutes. Remove it from the heat.

recipe continues

4. Using the whipping attachment on your mixer, whip the coconut fat into a cream. This will take 2 to 3 minutes on high speed. It should resemble a whipped cream made from heavy dairy cream.

5. Slowly and gently fold the almond butter mixture into the whipped cream.

6. Scoop the mousse into individual serving bowls and refrigerate until you're ready to serve it. The mousse should keep for about a week in the fridge.

Variations

* For an extra boost of almond flavor, add ½ teaspoon of almond extract.
* Chocolate lovers can use Chocolate Hazelnut Spread (page 34) in place of almond butter.
* For a great Thanksgiving treat, substitute pumpkin puree for the almond butter, and add 1 teaspoon of cinnamon, ¼ teaspoon of nutmeg, and ¼ teaspoon of ginger.

PREP AND CHILL TIME: About 30 minutes (not including the overnight refrigeration of the coconut milk)

Brownie Bars

IF YOU'RE A serious chocolate lover, look no further. The creamy taste of the macadamia nut butter in this recipe pairs so well with the richness of the chocolate chips, it's a match made in heaven, recreated in your kitchen. Beware—you might want to eat all of the brownies in one sitting, so it's best to have a buddy with you! If there are any left after twenty-four hours, you're better at self-control than I am.

MAKES NINE 2-INCH (5 CM) SQUARES

1 cup (100 g) gluten free rolled oats

1 cup (240 g) macadamia nut butter (see Basic Nut Butter recipe, page 26)

12 Medjool dates, pits removed

¾ cup (120 g) dark chocolate chips

2 tablespoons unsweetened cocoa powder

½ teaspoon sea salt

3 to 4 tablespoons water

1. Combine the oats and the macadamia nut butter in a food processor. Pulse until the mixture has a coarse consistency, about 2 minutes.

2. Add the rest of the ingredients except the water.

3. Grind for a minute, then slowly add the water 1 tablespoon at a time. You'll see the mixture begin to come together to form a thick batter.

4. Line an 8 x 8-inch (20 cm x 20 cm) glass dish with parchment paper. Make sure there is enough paper hanging off the sides so that you can easily pull the brownies out once they're firm.

recipe continues

5. Spoon the batter into the dish evenly. The batter will be extremely sticky, so it helps to wet the spatula first. After the batter is spread in the dish, place it in the fridge to set, about 1 hour.

6. When the brownies are firm, grab the sides of the parchment paper and pull the brownies out. Cut them into nine even squares using a pizza cutter or a sharp knife.

7. These bars must be stored in the refrigerator, where they will last for up to 2 weeks, or in the freezer for up to 6 months.

PREP AND CHILL TIME: About 65 minutes

Brownie Bars

Cookie Dough Balls

ONE MAJOR RITE of passage in childhood is eating raw cookie dough straight out of the mixing bowl. It's become so ingrained in American culture that you can even buy cookie dough candy and ice cream now. There's a catch to eating the homemade stuff, of course: as almost everyone knows, eating raw egg can be harmful. That's what makes this recipe so great—there's no egg in it! Eat these treats to your heart's content. The only thing that's ever unsatisfying about this dish is that it runs out so quickly!

MAKES FIFTEEN 1-INCH (2.5 CM) BALLS

1 cup (100 g) gluten-free oats

10 Medjool dates, pits removed

1 cup (240 g) macadamia nut butter (see Basic Nut Butter recipe, page 26)

1 teaspoon ground vanilla beans (see page xx)

2 tablespoons water

½ cup (80 g) dark chocolate chips

1. Blend the oats in a food processor until they are coarsely ground. This takes about 2 minutes.
2. Add the dates, macadamia nut butter, vanilla, and water. Pulse until a dough starts to form, 2 to 3 minutes.
3. Fold the chocolate chips into the dough, or use them in the next step to coat the outside of the balls.
4. Roll the dough into bite-size balls. If you're covering them with chocolate chips, roll the balls around on a plate of chocolate chips and then gently press the chips in.

recipe continues

5. Place the balls on a parchment-lined baking sheet. Stick the baking sheet into the fridge so that the balls can firm up, about 30 minutes.

6. Store the cookie dough balls in the refrigerator for up to 2 weeks, or in the freezer for up to 6 months.

NOTE

If you want to bump up the protein in this recipe, add 2 tablespoons of chia seeds, hemp seeds, or leftover nut milk pulp (see How to Use Nut Pulp, page 57).

PREP AND CHILL TIME: About 40 minutes

Chocolate Almond Banana Cups

THE *TODAY* SHOW on NBC featured this recipe as a "Too Good to Be Healthy" contest winner in February 2014. Once you make it, you'll see why. It's perfect for when you want a little bite of something sweet but don't want to indulge to the point of guilt. These cups are so delicious that one of the *Today* show's hosts even served them at her Super Bowl party—and from what I was told, they were quite the hit. With accolades like that, you can be sure you won't be disappointed.

MAKES TWELVE 2½-INCH (6.4 CM) PIECES

1 very ripe banana, mashed

⅓ cup (80 g) almond butter (see Basic Nut Butter recipe, page 26)

½ teaspoon ground vanilla beans or vanilla extract (see page xx)

4.5 ounces (125 g) dark chocolate or ⅓ cup (80 g) chocolate chips

¼ cup (60ml) almond milk (see Basic Nut Milk recipe, page 3)

1. Mix together the banana, almond butter, and vanilla in a small bowl.

2. Mix the chocolate and the milk in a double boiler (see Notes on the following page). Heat and keep stirring until the chocolate is melted and very smooth, about 5 minutes.

3. Pour a small amount of chocolate into the bottom of a lined muffin cup. Once you have a little chocolate in the bottom of each cup, place the muffin pan in the freezer to set, 5 to 10 minutes.

4. When the chocolate is firm, spoon a little dollop of the banana mixture into each cup, on top of the

recipe continues

chocolate. Once all the cups have an even amount of banana mixture, fill them with the remaining chocolate and place them in the freezer to set. This should take a few hours.

5. Serve immediately after removing them from the freezer (see Notes below). These will last for up to 6 months frozen.

NOTES

* To create a double boiler, fill a medium saucepan with water. Bring the water to a boil, then place a heatproof glass bowl on top of the pot. Add the chocolate chips and nut milk to the glass bowl. This will allow you to gently melt the chocolate without burning it.

* There are two things to note about storing these cups: First, they must be kept in the freezer, or else the banana gets too mushy. Second, they melt very quickly once out of the freezer, so only pull them out right before you intend to eat them.

Variation

You can go the simple route with this recipe and fill the cups with the banana, almond butter, and vanilla mixture only. It makes a delightfully healthy snack that is lower in calories and fat.

PREP AND CHILL TIME: About 3 hours

Chocolate Almond Banana Cups

Baked Treats

I love to bake. In fact, I've enjoyed baking since I was a kid, mainly because I love sweets. Over the years I've refined my craft, and the little girl inside me still enjoys eating the goodies I create. The following recipes represent some of my favorite things not only to bake, but also to devour. None of them are difficult to make, and nut butters always satisfy my sweet tooth. All of the delectable treats in this chapter will fill your kitchen with great aromas and will taste even better than they smell. Don't forget to wash them down with a glass of nut milk!

Almond Joy Cookies

IF YOU'RE A fan of Almond Joys, you'll love these cookies. They're even much better than the candy bar, because they won't spike your blood sugar and cause you to come crashing down, craving more sugar. These cookies include all the flavors of an Almond Joy—without the guilt. Naturally sweetened and gluten-free, they're worth every bite. Try them out and see for yourself.

MAKES TWELVE 2-INCH (5 CM) COOKIES

1 tablespoon flax meal

3 tablespoons warm water

1½ cups (135 g) gluten-free oat flour (see page xxii)

½ cup (45 g) shredded unsweetened coconut

1 teaspoon baking powder

1 teaspoon sea salt

½ cup (120 g) almond butter (see Basic Nut Butter recipe, page 26)

⅓ cup (80ml) pure maple syrup

¼ cup (60ml) coconut oil (see page xix)

1 teaspoon ground vanilla beans or vanilla extract (see page xx)

½ teaspoon almond extract

1.75 ounces (50g) dark chocolate, roughly chopped, or ½ cup (80 g) dark chocolate chips

1. Preheat the oven to 350°F (175°C).

2. Whisk together the flax meal and water in a small bowl. Place it in the refrigerator for a minute to set. It will become gummy, like an egg.

3. Mix the oat flour, coconut, baking powder, and sea salt in a large bowl. Set it aside.

4. Mix the almond butter, maple syrup, coconut oil, vanilla, and almond extract in a small saucepan. Stir over medium heat until smooth, about a minute or so.

5. When the almond butter mixture is smooth, add it to the bowl of dry ingredients. Mix well, 1 to 2 minutes, using either a handheld or stand mixer (both work well).

recipe continues

6. Add the flax/water mixture and stir the ingredients until they are well combined. Fold in the chocolate.

7. Using a small cookie scoop or rolling the dough into bite-size balls, place the dough on a parchment-lined baking sheet at least 1 inch (2.5 cm) apart from one another. Bake for 12 minutes, or until the cookies start to brown around the edges.

8. Let the cookies completely cool on the baking sheet before storing them in an airtight container. Store in the refrigerator for up to 3 weeks or in the freezer for up to 6 months. If frozen, let them thaw at room temperature for about 5 minutes before eating.

PREP AND BAKE TIME: About 20 minutes

Almond Butter Sandwich Cookies

SANDWICH COOKIES COME in many shapes and forms. When you make your own, you can create whatever flavor combos come to mind. In this case, I combined my beloved almond butter with a decadent chocolate spread. The outcome is pure heaven in your mouth. Once you see how easy this is, you'll want to make even more new flavor fusions.

MAKES SIXTEEN 1-INCH (2.5 CM) COOKIES

1 tablespoon flax meal

3 tablespoons warm water

2 cups (180 g) gluten-free oat flour (see page xxii)

½ cup (115 g) coconut sugar

1 teaspoon ground vanilla beans (see page xx)

½ teaspoon sea salt

1 cup plus 2 tablespoons (270 g) almond butter (see Basic Nut Butter recipe, page 26)

¾ cup (180 ml) almond milk (see Basic Nut Milk recipe, page 3)

½ cup (125 g) Chocolate Peanut Butter Spread (page 38)

1. Preheat the oven to 350°F (175°C).

2. Whisk together the flax meal and water in a small bowl. Place it in the refrigerator for a minute to set. It will become gummy, like an egg.

3. Mix together the oat flour, coconut sugar, vanilla, and sea salt in a large bowl. Set it aside.

4. Mix the almond butter and milk in a small saucepan. Stir over medium heat until the ingredients are well combined, 1 to 2 minutes. Remove from the heat.

5. Add the almond butter mixture to the bowl of dry ingredients and mix for 1 to 2 minutes, until the ingredients are well combined,

recipe continues

using either a handheld or stand mixer (both work well).

6. Add the flax/water mixture and continue to mix for another minute.

7. Form the cookies into bite-size balls, using either your hands or a cookie scoop, and place them on a parchment-lined or greased baking sheet, about ½ inch (1.3 cm) apart. You should have 32 balls. Flatten each cookie with your palm.

8. Bake for 10 to 11 minutes. It's hard to visually tell when these are done, so I lightly press my finger into a cookie to feel if it's firm enough. Let the cookies completely cool before removing them from the baking sheet.

9. Once the cookies are cool, spread some Chocolate Peanut Butter Spread onto one, and then make a sandwich by putting another cookie on top. Repeat these steps until all the sandwich cookies are made.

10. Set the cookies in the fridge to firm up, about 30 minutes.

11. Store them in the refrigerator for up to 2 weeks, or in the freezer for up to 6 months.

NOTES

* You can substitute vanilla extract for the ground vanilla beans. I just happen to love the strong, fresh flavor of the vanilla beans.

* You can use a regular large egg in place of the flax meal and water if you like.

Variations

* A fun flavor combination is to use your favorite homemade jam (see page 78) instead of the chocolate spread.

* Coconut butter (see page xxii) works well in the middle, too.

PREP AND BAKE TIME: About 50 minutes

Almond Butter Sandwich Cookies

Peanut Butter and Chocolate Brownies

THESE THICK, FUDGY brownies are the ultimate indulgence. I call for dark chocolate as well as unsweetened cocoa powder to make them extra-rich. When you add cashew butter to the mix, it takes these brownies to the next level.

MAKES NINE 2-INCH (5 CM) BROWNIES

1 tablespoon flax meal

3 tablespoons warm water

2 cups (180 g) gluten-free oat flour (see page xxii)

½ cup (60 g) unsweetened cocoa powder

1½ teaspoons baking powder

½ teaspoon sea salt

1 cup (250 g) Classic Peanut Butter (page 29)

1.75 ounces (50g) dark chocolate or ½ cup (80 g) dark chocolate chips

½ cup (120 ml) almond milk (see Basic Nut Milk recipe, page 3)

½ cup (120 ml) pure maple syrup

½ cup (120 ml) coconut oil (see page xix)

¼ cup (60 ml) unsweetened applesauce (see page xviii)

1 teaspoon ground vanilla beans or vanilla extract (see page xx)

1. Preheat the oven to 350°F (175°C).

2. Whisk together the flax meal and warm water in a small bowl. Place it in the refrigerator for a minute to set. It will become gummy, like an egg.

3. Mix the oat flour, cocoa powder, baking powder, and sea salt in a large bowl and set it aside.

4. Mix the remaining ingredients in a small saucepan. Stir constantly with a silicone spatula over medium heat until the ingredients are well combined, about 5 minutes.

5. Add the mixture from the saucepan to the bowl of dry ingredients and mix until well combined, 1 to 2 minutes, using either a handheld or stand mixer (both work well).

recipe continues

6. Add the flax/water mixture and mix until the ingredients are well combined, about 1 minute.

7. Line an 8 x 8-inch (20 cm x 20 cm) glass baking dish with parchment paper. Make sure there is enough paper hanging off the sides so that you can easily remove the brownies after baking.

8. Spoon the batter evenly into the baking dish, pressing it down firmly. Bake for 15 minutes, or until a toothpick inserted into the middle comes out clean. I like mine extra-moist so that they're a little gooey in the middle, but if you prefer a more cake-like brownie, you can bake them for an additional 5 minutes.

9. Wait until the brownies are completely cooled before removing them from the baking dish. To remove the brownies, simply grab the extra parchment paper at the sides and lift them out of the baking dish. Cut the brownies into nine even squares using a pizza cutter or a sharp knife.

10. Store the brownies in an airtight container in the refrigerator for up to 2 weeks or in the freezer for up to 6 months. When I'm ready to eat one out of the freezer, I let it thaw at room temperature for an hour or two. You can also thaw them in a microwave using the defrost setting.

NOTE

If this recipe calls for more oil than you care to use, you can cut it down to ¼ cup (60 ml) and add an extra ¼ cup (60 ml) of applesauce or non-dairy plain yogurt.

PREP AND BAKE TIME:
25 to 30 minutes

Chocolate Chip Macadamia Cookies

WHEN I SWITCHED to a healthier diet, I thought chocolate chip cookies were out of my reach. Well, my friends, I'm here to tell you that's not true. Macadamia butter is so naturally buttery that it does a superb job of mimicking the taste and texture of dairy in a more traditional chocolate chip cookie recipe. There's very little oil in this recipe, but it'll never taste dry, thanks to the macadamias.

MAKES TWENTY-TWO 1-INCH (2.5 CM) COOKIES

2 tablespoons flax meal

¼ cup plus 2 tablespoons warm water

2¾ cups (248 g) gluten-free oat flour (see page xxii)

½ cup (47 g) shredded unsweetened coconut

2 teaspoons ground vanilla beans (see page xx)

1 teaspoon baking powder

1 teaspoon baking soda

½ teaspoon sea salt

¾ cup (180 g) macadamia butter (see Basic Nut Butter recipe, page 26)

½ cup (120 ml) pure maple syrup

2 tablespoons coconut oil (see page xix)

½ cup (80 g) chocolate chips

1. Preheat the oven to 350°F (175°C).
2. Whisk together the flax meal and water in a small bowl. Place it in the refrigerator for a minute to set. It will become gummy, like an egg.
3. Mix the flour, coconut, vanilla, baking powder, baking soda, and sea salt in a large bowl and set it aside.
4. Mix the macadamia butter, maple syrup, and coconut oil in a small saucepan. Stir over medium heat with a silicone spatula until the ingredients are well combined, about 5 minutes. Add the mixture to the bowl of dry ingredients.
5. Add the flax meal/water mixture and mix until the ingredients are

recipe continues

well combined, about 1 minute, using either a handheld or stand mixer (both work well).

6. Fold in the chocolate chips using a spatula, then place the bowl of dough in the fridge for 20 minutes to firm up.

7. Drop tablespoons of the dough onto a parchment-lined baking sheet about 1 inch (2.5 cm) apart from one another. Bake for 10 to 12 min-utes, or until the edges look slightly golden. Make sure the cookies are completely cooled before removing them from the baking sheet.

8. Store the cookies in the refrigerator for up to 2 weeks, or in the freezer for up to 6 months.

PREP AND BAKE TIME: About 45 minutes

Chocolate Chip Macadamia Cookies

Chocolate Cashew Butter Thumbprint Cookies

WHEN I THINK of thumbprint cookies, I picture a buttery cookie with a crisp outside and a chewy center. Cashew butter is very rich and creamy in texture, making it the perfect ingredient to use in these thumbprint cookies. I filled them with chocolate here, but you can also use homemade jam or even a different nut butter.

MAKES EIGHTEEN 1-INCH (2.5 CM) COOKIES

1 cup (135 g) cashew butter (see Basic Nut Butter recipe, page 26)

½ cup (120 ml) pure maple syrup

¼ cup (60 ml) almond milk (see Basic Nut Milk recipe, page 3)

2 tablespoons coconut oil (see page xix)

2 teaspoons ground vanilla beans or vanilla extract (see page xx)

1½ cups (135 g) gluten-free oat flour (see page xxii)

½ teaspoon baking powder

½ teaspoon sea salt

½ cup (80 g) dark chocolate chips (see Note on the following page)

1. Preheat the oven to 350°F (175°C).

2. Mix the cashew butter, maple syrup, almond milk, coconut oil, and vanilla in a small saucepan. Stir over medium heat until the ingredients are smooth and well combined, 2 to 3 minutes. Remove the mixture from the heat and let it cool to room temperature.

3. While the mixture in the saucepan cools, mix together the oat flour, baking powder, and sea salt in a medium bowl.

4. Once the cashew butter mixture is cooled, add it to the bowl of dry ingredients. Using either a hand

recipe continues

held or stand mixer, mix until the ingredients are well combined, about 2 minutes, You might need to scrape down the sides of the bowl a few times.

5. Drop bite-size dollops of batter onto a parchment-lined baking sheet about 1 inch (2.5 cm) apart, using either two spoons or a cookie scoop. Since this batter is thick and sticky, I prefer the cookie scoop.

6. Press your thumb into the center of each cookie, then add the chocolate chips into the indentation. I put 5 to 6 chocolate chips into each thumbprint. This step provides a great opportunity for small children to help—my kids love to do this. They also love to sneak chocolate chips!

7. Bake the cookies for 10 to 12 minutes, until slightly golden around the edges. Let them cool completely before removing them from the baking sheets.

8. Store the cookies in an airtight container in the refrigerator, where they should last 7 to 10 days, or in the freezer for up to 6 months.

NOTE

For the dark chocolate in this recipe, I use 63 percent cacao as opposed to my normal 72 percent (see page xviii), since I think the slightly sweeter taste works better here, but you can use any kind you like.

Variation

To switch up this recipe, you can substitute ¼ cup (85 g) of your favorite jam for the chocolate. See page 78 for Homemade Jam that's perfect to use in these thumbprint cookies.

PREP AND BAKE TIME:
20 to 25 minutes

Flourless Almond Butter Blondies

MUCH LIKE THE Chocolate Chip Macadamia Cookies (page 159), these blondies have a rich and buttery taste without any oil, flour, or dairy products. They also have a surprise element: chickpeas, which work really well in sweet dishes. My kids were totally fooled—they had no idea that a secret healthy ingredient was hiding in these treats. Neither did my husband. I actually use chickpeas quite often in the kitchen, sometimes roasting them with a touch of maple syrup and cinnamon for a quick sweet treat.

MAKES NINE 2-INCH (5 CM) SQUARES

1 cup (200 g) dried or one 14-ounce (480 ml) can chickpeas

1 tablespoon flax meal

3 tablespoons warm water

1 cup (100 g) gluten-free rolled oats

½ teaspoon sea salt

1 cup (250 g) almond butter (see Basic Nut Butter recipe, page 26)

½ cup (120 ml) pure maple syrup

½ cup (50 g) shredded unsweetened coconut

1 teaspoon vanilla extract

½ cup (80 g) dark chocolate chips

1. Preheat the oven to 350°F (175°C).

2. If you're using dried chickpeas, soak them overnight, rinse them, and then boil them until they are soft. If you are using canned chickpeas, drain them, then rinse well and pat them dry.

3. Whisk together the flax meal and water in a small bowl. Place it in the refrigerator for a minute to set. It will become gummy, like an egg.

4. Combine the chickpeas, oats, and sea salt in a food processor. Mix them slightly, about 1 minute.

5. Add the almond butter, maple syrup, coconut, vanilla, and flax/

recipe continues

water mixture. Continue to pulse the food processor until the ingredients are well mixed, 2 to 3 minutes. You might have to stop and scrape down the sides of the canister a few times.

6. Line an 8 x 8-inch (20 cm x 20 cm) glass baking dish with parchment paper. Make sure there is enough paper hanging off the sides so that you can easily remove the blondies after baking.

7. Carefully spoon the batter into the baking dish. You might need to wet the spatula, because the dough will be very sticky. Make sure the batter is pressed down evenly.

8. Sprinkle the chocolate chips on top and gently press them into the blondies. Bake them for about 20 minutes. To tell when these are done, carefully touch your finger to the top to see if they're firm, which means they're ready to come out of the oven.

9. Let the blondies cool completely before removing them from the baking dish. To remove them, grab the parchment paper that's sticking out and carefully lift the whole thing out of the pan. Cut the blondies into nine even squares using a pizza cutter or a sharp knife.

10. Store them in an airtight container in the refrigerator for 7 to 10 days, or in the freezer for up to 6 months. When you want to enjoy some blondies that have been frozen, it's best to thaw them at room temperature. Because of the chocolate chips on the top, reheating them in the microwave might make a mess.

NOTE

You can use white beans in place of chickpeas if you prefer the taste; both work well in this recipe.

PREP AND BAKE TIME: About 30 minutes, not including the overnight soak if using dried chickpeas

**Flourless Almond
Butter Blondies**

Slow Cooker Peanut Butter Granola Bars

THE SLOW COOKER shouldn't be reserved just for soups and chili; you can actually use it for many other things, such as these granola bars. Cooking food slowly allows for far greater flavor to develop. In the summer the slow cooker can come in quite handy when you don't want to heat up your whole kitchen with the oven. The best part? You don't even need to be home to make these soft and chewy granola bars!

MAKES TEN 3 X 1-INCH (7.5 X 2.5 CM) BARS

1 cup (250 g) Classic Peanut Butter (page 29)

½ cup (120 ml) pure maple syrup

2 tablespoons almond milk (see Basic Nut Milk recipe, page 3)

2 teaspoons vanilla extract

2 cups (200 g) gluten-free rolled oats

¼ cup (35 g) flax meal

¼ cup (25 g) unsweetened shredded coconut

2 tablespoons chia seeds

½ teaspoon sea salt

½ cup (80 g) dark chocolate chips

1. Mix the peanut butter, maple syrup, almond milk, and vanilla in a saucepan. Stir over medium heat until the ingredients are well combined, about 5 minutes. Remove from the heat and let the mixture cool to room temperature.

2. While the peanut butter mixture cools, mix together the oats, flax meal, coconut, chia seeds, and sea salt in a large bowl.

3. Add the mixture from the saucepan to the dry ingredients and stir until well combined, about 1 minute, using either a handheld or stand mixer (both work well).

recipe continues

4. Fold in the chocolate chips using a spatula or wooden spoon.

5. Line the slow cooker with parchment paper, making sure there is enough paper to hang off the sides so that you can easily lift out the bars once they're cooked. Brush the parchment paper with a little coconut oil.

6. Spoon the mixture into the bottom of the slow cooker, pressing it down evenly. It's important to pack the mixture down firmly to make sure the bars hold together.

7. Set the slow cooker on low and cook for 1½ to 2½ hours. Everyone's slow cooker seems to run at a different temperature, and older ones are known to run hotter. You'll know that the granola bars are done when the middle no longer seems mushy. When they're done, lift them out by grabbing the parchment paper that's hanging off the sides. Set them aside to cool for about 25 minutes. If you cut the bars before they've fully cooled, they might crumble.

8. Once the mixture is completely cooled, use a pizza cutter or a sharp knife to make 3 x 1-inch (7.5 cm x 2.5 cm) bars.

9. Store these in a container with a sheet of parchment paper in between each bar. If you want to be thrifty, you can use the same parchment that you cooked them in. They will last at room temperature for up to 4 days, in the refrigerator for up to 3 weeks, or in the freezer for up to 6 months.

Variations

There are lots of variations for this recipe. You can add any kind of dried fruit, seeds, chopped nuts, or even cacao nibs. I suggest ¼ cup of any of those items for a change of taste.

PREP AND COOK TIME: About 3½ hours

ICE CREAM

If you have certain dietary limitations (such as being gluten- or dairy-free), finding an affordable store-bought ice cream can be almost impossible—and very expensive. Here's a good alternative: make scrumptious frozen treats in the comfort of your own home. Most of these recipes require an ice cream machine, which will pay for itself after only a few batches, plus you'll have the power to control the ingredients and create whatever flavor your heart desires. Once you begin making ice cream and see how fun it is, you'll find yourself constantly thinking of new variations to try. This was by far one of my favorite sections to put together, especially when it came to sampling the results!

Three-Ingredient Peanut Butter Ice Cream

THIS RECIPE PROVIDES a great intro to making your own ice cream. It's simple, with very few ingredients, yet comes out tasting superb.

MAKES FOUR ½-CUP (120 ML) SERVINGS

One 14-ounce (400 ml) can full-fat coconut milk (see Note on the following page)

1 cup (250 g) Classic Peanut Butter (page 29)

3 tablespoons pure maple syrup

Optional add-ins: 2 tablespoons chocolate chips, nuts, or dried fruit

1. Chill your ice cream machine's bowl in the freezer for at least 18 hours before making this recipe.

2. Combine all the ingredients in a blender and blend for 1 to 2 minutes.

3. Pour the mixture into your ice cream machine and follow the manufacturer's instructions. It should take about 20 minutes until the ice cream is ready. When the ice cream has about 5 minutes left, add the optional add-ins of your choice if desired. This ice cream will have a soft-serve consistency. If you like a harder ice cream, stick the mixture into the freezer for another hour or two before you eat it.

4. Eat the ice cream immediately, or store it in the freezer for up to

recipe continues

6 months. Since it doesn't contain any emulsifiers or additives, homemade ice cream will get very hard when frozen. If you plan to eat it after storing it in the freezer, pull it out about 45 minutes before serving to make sure it's soft enough to scoop.

NOTES

* Make sure to use canned coconut milk, not the coconut milk that comes in a carton. The milk in cartons has a far lower fat content, so the ice cream will come out rather icy (see page xix).

* Sunflower Seed Butter (page 55) or any other nut butter can be substituted for peanut butter in this recipe.
* If you don't have an ice cream machine, you can mix everything in a blender, pour it into ice cube trays, and then blend it again once the mixture is frozen.

PREP AND CHILL TIME: About 25 minutes, or up to 2 hours for a harder ice cream (not counting the 18 hours the ice cream machine's bowl needs to chill beforehand)

Chocolate Hazelnut Ice Cream

CHOCOLATE AND HAZELNUTS are always a winning combination. As soon as I mention those two words together, I'll bet your mind instantly conjures up an image of that famous chocolate hazelnut spread. What if you could have that taste without all the additives, in the form of a decadent ice cream? Well, here you go! You'll never believe there's only 2 tablespoons of added sugar in this entire batch.

MAKES FOUR ½-CUP (75 G) SERVINGS

One 14-ounce (400 ml) can full-fat coconut milk (Note on the following page)

1 cup (240 g) Chocolate Hazelnut Spread (page 34)

2 tablespoons pure maple syrup

½ teaspoon sea salt

1. Chill your ice cream machine's bowl in the freezer for at least 18 hours before making this recipe.

2. Mix all the ingredients together in a high-powered blender for 2 to 3 minutes.

3. Pour the mixture into your ice cream machine and follow the manufacturer's instructions. It should take about 20 minutes until the ice cream is ready. This ice cream will have a soft-serve consistency. If you like a harder ice cream, stick the mixture into the freezer for an extra hour or two before you eat it.

4. Eat the ice cream immediately, or store it in the freezer for up to

recipe continues

6 months. Since it doesn't contain any emulsifiers or additives, homemade ice cream will get very hard when frozen. If you plan to eat it after storing it in the freezer, pull it out about 45 minutes before serving to make sure it's soft enough to scoop.

NOTE

Make sure to use canned coconut milk, not the coconut milk that comes in a carton (see page xix).

PREP AND CHILL TIME: About 25 minutes, or up to 2 hours for a harder ice cream (not counting the 18 hours the ice cream machine's bowl needs to chill beforehand)

Chocolate Hazelnut Ice Cream

Pistachio Ice Cream

NO MATTER THE weather, sometimes a girl just needs a bowl of ice cream, and pistachio is an excellent flavor to choose. Eating the little nuts all by themselves can be like a game of hide-and-seek—if you can get that darn shell off, you've won. So for this recipe, even though they cost a bit more, I suggest buying pistachios that have already been shelled. It will drastically reduce your preparation time and save your fingers for spooning up this delicious ice cream.

MAKES FOUR ½-CUP (75 G) SERVINGS

One 14-ounce (400 ml) can full fat coconut milk (see page xix)

1½ cups (190 g) raw, unsalted pistachios, plus 2 tablespoons for mixing into the ice cream for crunch

2 to 3 tablespoons pure maple syrup

½ teaspoon sea salt

1. Chill your ice cream machine's bowl in the freezer for at least 18 hours before making this recipe.

2. Mix together the coconut milk, 1½ cups (190 g) of pistachios, maple syrup, and sea salt in a high-powered blender for 2 to 3 minutes.

3. Pour the contents into your ice cream machine and follow the manufacturer's instructions. It should take about 20 minutes until the ice cream is ready.

4. When the ice cream has about 5 minutes left, sprinkle the 2 table-spoons of extra pistachios into the ice cream to add some crunch. You

recipe continues

might need to gently guide the ice cream as it spins in the machine to make sure the pistachios are thoroughly mixed in. I use a silicone spatula for this. This ice cream will have a soft-serve consistency. If you like a harder ice cream, stick the mix into the freezer for another hour or two before you eat it.

5. Eat the ice cream immediately, or store it in the freezer for up to 6 months. Since it doesn't contain any emulsifiers or additives, homemade ice cream will get very hard when frozen. If you plan to eat it after storing it in the freezer, pull it out about 45 minutes before serving to make sure it's soft enough to scoop.

NOTE

If you don't have an ice cream machine, try blending everything together in a blender and then pouring the mixture into ice cube trays. Once the ice cube trays are frozen, blend them in the blender for a treat similar to soft-serve ice cream.

PREP AND CHILL TIME: About 30 minutes, or up to 2 hours for a harder ice cream (not counting the 18 hours the ice cream machine's bowl needs to chill beforehand)

Chocolate Peanut Butter Chunk Ice Cream

I TYPICALLY MAKE all of my ice creams using full-fat coconut milk as a base, but this recipe is a bit different. Since homemade Brazil nut milk is so creamy, I decided to try it in an ice cream recipe. The texture is a little different from ice cream made with coconut milk; it's rather similar to a sorbet. The flavor definitely isn't lacking, with a big chocolate punch and peanut butter chunks scattered around like little bites of heaven.

MAKES FOUR ½-CUP (75 G) SERVINGS

2 cups (480 ml) Brazil nut milk (see Basic Nut Milk recipe, page 3)

1 cup (160 g) dark chocolate chips

2 to 3 tablespoons unsweetened cocoa powder or cacao powder

2 tablespoons pure maple syrup

1 teaspoon vanilla extract

½ cup (125 g) Classic Peanut Butter (page 29)

1. Chill your ice cream machine's bowl in the freezer for at least 18 hours before making this recipe.

2. Combine the Brazil nut milk, chocolate chips, cocoa powder, maple syrup, and vanilla in a high-powered blender. Blend for 1 to 2 minutes on high, until well mixed.

3. Pour the mixture into your ice cream machine and follow the manufacturer's instructions. It should take about 20 minutes until the ice cream is ready. When the ice cream has about 5 minutes left, start dropping chunks of peanut

recipe continues

butter into the machine as it runs. There's really no measurement for this; it just depends on how big or small you like your chunks to be. You might need to help guide the ice cream as it spins in the machine to make sure that all the chunks of peanut butter are distributed evenly; I use a silicone spatula for this. When the ice cream is ready, it will have a soft-serve consistency. If you like a harder ice cream, stick the mixture into the freezer for another hour or two before you're going to eat it.

4. Eat the ice cream immediately, or store it in the freezer for up to 6 months. Since it doesn't contain any emulsifiers or additives, home-made ice cream will get very hard when frozen. If you plan to eat it after storing in the freezer, pull it out about 45 minutes before serving to make sure it's soft enough to scoop.

NOTE

Feel free to substitute another nut butter for the peanut butter if you wish. You can also try Sunflower Seed Butter (page 155).

PREP AND CHILL TIME: About 25 minutes, or up to 2 hours for a harder ice cream (not counting the 18 hours the ice cream machine's bowl needs to chill beforehand)

Chocolate Peanut Butter
Chunk Ice Cream

Banana Macadamia Ice Cream

I LOVE MAKING ice cream with bananas, especially since there are several benefits: less fat and sugar, and no ice cream maker is necessary. For those who have allergies, rest assured that this recipe is also dairy-free. When you freeze a banana, it becomes incredibly rich and silky in texture. It's actually quite amazing. I buy two bunches of bananas each week, and one goes directly into the freezer for smoothies and ice cream.

MAKES THREE ½-CUP (75 G) SERVINGS

3 frozen bananas (see Note on the following page)

2 tablespoons macadamia nut butter (see Basic Nut Butter recipe, page 26)

1 to 2 tablespoons almond milk (see Basic Nut Milk recipe, page 3)

1. Slice the frozen bananas into thin slices. Put them in a high-powered blender with the other ingredients. Blend for 1 to 2 minutes, scraping down the sides a few times. You might need to add a bit more almond milk to achieve the consistency you desire.

2. Once you see the mixture become a soft-serve consistency, it's ready. If you like a harder ice cream, stick it into the freezer for about an hour or two before serving.

3. Eat the ice cream immediately, or store it in the freezer for up to 6 months. Since it doesn't contain any emulsifiers or additives,

recipe continues

homemade ice cream will get very hard when frozen. If you plan to eat it after storing in the freezer, pull it out about 45 minutes before serving to make sure it's soft enough to scoop.

Variations

* Feel free to add whatever toppings you like: chopped nuts, cacao nibs, dried fruit, chocolate chips. The possibilities are endless.

* A fun thing to do with the kids is create your own sundae bar. Spoon a scoop of ice cream into each bowl and set out some toppings for them to choose.

PREP AND CHILL TIME: About 5 minutes, or up to an hour for a harder texture

Resources

Ingredient Retailers

Bob's Red Mill Natural Foods
bobsredmill.com
  Gluten-free oat flour, rolled oats, coconut flour, flaxseeds and flax meal; nuts and seeds; unsweetened shredded coconut

Cocoa Supply
cocoasupply.com
  Cacao nibs, cocoa butter, chia seeds, vanilla beans

EatRaw
eatraw.com
  Bulk nuts and seeds, cacao nibs and powder, cocoa butter, coconut butter, goji berries

Nuts.com
nuts.com
  Bulk nuts and seeds; cacao butter, nibs, and powder; carob chips; cocoa butter; coconut milk, oil, and sugar; chia seeds; dates; flaxseeds and flax meal; gluten-free coconut flour and rolled oats; goji berries; raw honey; unsweetened shredded coconut; vanilla beans

Sunfood Superfoods
sunfood.com
  Bulk nuts and seeds; cacao butter, nibs, and powder; coconut oil and sugar; dates; goji berries; raw honey; vanilla powder

True Foods Market
truefoodsmarket.com
  Bulk nuts and seeds; cacao nibs and powder; chia seeds; coconut flour, oil, and sugar; dates; Ener-G Egg Replacer; flaxseeds and flax meal; gluten-free rolled oats and coconut flour; goji berries; pure maple syrup; raw honey; vanilla powder

Vitacost

vitacost.com

Cacao nibs and powder; carob chips; cocoa butter; coconut butter, flour, milk, oil, and sugar; dates; Endangered Species Chocolate bars; Ener-G Egg Replacer; Enjoy Life chocolate chips; flaxseeds and flax meal; gluten-free rolled oats, oat flour, and coconut flour; goji berries; nuts and seeds; pure maple syrup; raw honey; unsweetened applesauce and shredded coconut; vanilla beans .

Kindred Spirits

I have been inspired by many talented bloggers, including:

* Angela Liddon, creator of *Oh She Glows* (ohsheglows.com)

* Emily von Euw, creator of *This Rawsome Vegan Life* (thisrawsomeveganlife.com)

* Katie Higgins, creator of *Chocolate Covered Katie* (chocolatecoveredkatie.com)

* Kiersten Frase, creator of *Oh My Veggies* (ohmyveggies.com)

Acknowledgments

First and foremost, I would like to thank my husband, Marcus, for his support. He has been there from day one, helping me with the edits and also taste-testing the recipes.

Thank you to my in-laws, Steve and Heidi, for watching the girls for countless hours as I wrote this book.

Thank you to everyone who tested these recipes for me. Your feedback was very helpful.

Thank you to my editors at The Experiment, Molly Cavanaugh and Sasha Tropp, for helping me every step of the way. Thanks also to Pauline Neuwirth for her wonderful book design.

Lastly, thank you to my loyal readers. I appreciate each and every one of you. Without your support, this book and my blog, *My Whole Food Life*, would not be possible.

Index

About the Author

Melissa King is the writer, photographer, and recipe developer for the popular blog *My Whole Food Life*, at www.mywholefoodlife.com. Her recipes have been featured on the *Today* show, *iVillage*, *Greatist*, and *Popsugar Moms*. Melissa lives in Dallas, Texas, with her husband and two girls.